The Jobs of My Life

Bo Lanzi

Library of Congress Cataloging-in-Publication Data

ISBN: 97817300795008

Dedication

THIS BOOK IS dedicated to my lovely wife and beautiful daughter and all the good people I had the pleasure to meet during my working life.

Table of Contents

The Jobs

Forward

THIS IS NOT a "get rich quick" book, although I have carved out a decent living with my journey throughout my working life. This book does provide the reader with guidelines for finding a path toward a fulfilling employment life. Most of us will spend a third of our lives in jobs or positions of employment that may or may not be positive experiences, just steps toward a chance at finding our niche in the working world.

Through my life's memoirs attached to the many jobs I obtained during my employment journey, I have provided the reader with advice, recommendations, and suggestions of what to do and what to look out for when you are searching for a new job or are floundering in an existing one. I also have presented supervisor/management styles that I have witnessed through years of working in a variety of environments. I have related my opinions of what type of administrative methods best serve all concerned, including not only the management perspective, but also the front line employee's viewpoint.

Through the stories of my adventures in the working world, from my first ever job to my last position before retirement; I have encompassed fifty years of personal successes and pitfalls that actually occurred in my real life. Ninety percent of the stories and anecdotes that I have related in this book are true and real to the best of my knowledge. The other ten percent were either lapses in memory or just words added for the flow of the narrative.

Several of the jobs in the beginning of the book are menial or common and were short in time and content. However, they served to establish the backbone of my personality growth and demeanor. The positions that were longer in term and perseverance served as a basis of my self worth and assuredness. I mention "self-actualization" several times in the book as a goal that I attempted to attain during certain periods of my working life. My idea of achieving self-actualization is when one finally learns who they are and what they are about and reaches the true potential that is in all of us.

There were many obstacles in my working life that delayed my realization of this goal. However, I learned from my mistakes, advanced in knowledge from the negatives, grew in self-confidence even through difficult times, and continued to increase in self-worth until I achieved my self-actualization objective. It wasn't easy, and it took almost forty years of my life to accomplish, but it was well worth the wait.

My rationalization for completing this book was to "pass on" to the reader my knowledge through experiences in my working journey of the pitfalls and "bumps in the road" that will inevitably be part of everyone's path in life. Take on the challenges that are presented to you, fight through the adversities, do not accept failure, and become the out-standing individual that you know is inside of you.

Explore the possibilities, and be the best you can be. Enjoy the read.

Chapter One

The Early Years

Soft Pretzel Seller

EVERY JOB, NO matter how important or menial, will have circumstances, good or bad, and selling soft pretzels in the back yards of South Philly started off my life's jobs.

Three little dudes, myself included, about eight years old or so began selling soft pretzels. One of the kids' dads owned a small pretzel factory and gave us an amount of small and regular-sized pretzels (mostly factory rejects) to sell for profit. We would take turns walking around the neighborhood with the owner's kid and shout out, "Soooooooooft Prettttttttttzels!" throughout our little kingdom. Neighbors would actually come out and purchase our delicious eatables, with mustard upon request, from our four-wheel wagon for five to ten cents each. Some days were better than others, but we always had some left over change to be distributed to the three participants of our intimate business arrangement. However, as you will find, in many of my future endeavors throughout my life, excitement of new adventures in the working world would soon shed disappointment even in the most minor situation as a pretzel seller. It's not really clear because so many years have passed, but I know I was somehow being "ripped off" when the profits were disbursed. My dissatisfaction went to no avail with my other two partners. I was then left to tell my mom, who called their moms. The result was the end of my first job and business venture and the beginning of many more discouraging outcomes with the jobs of my life.

After leaving my first position, I remember feeling regret that I could not resolve the situation on my own. At a very young age, I realized that I must fend for myself against those who I felt were less than favorable to my well-being. Although, we were to remain friends for many years beyond this development, I still remember my feelings of bitterness whenever I heard the words, "Soooooooooft Prettttttttttzels"!!

Paper Boy

Another boyhood job, which back in the day was a very popular spot for adolescents, was to establish a paper route and deliver the daily newspaper to several homes in our neighborhood. I shared the responsibilities with my brother who is four years my elder. Although it didn't last long,

I once again began with excitement about making decent cash for my age with the help of my family. My brother and I elected to deliver the late edition *Bulletin* so we would not have to get up really early and deliver the other Philly newspaper, the *Inquirer*.

Initially, everything went fairly well. My dad became an integral part of our venture by driving us to the newspaper station and then picking us up after our delivery responsibilities were over. For the most part, this became an enjoyable routine—until the collection period came along, which was once a month. My brother and I would go door-to-door requesting the monthly payment for the paper delivery. Most neighbors would pay without hesitation, but some would either not respond to our knocking or flat out tell us they did not have the money to pay us. It got to a point that we were not making much money at all because we were charged for the papers whether we received reimbursement or not. Of course, my dad got involved, and let's say his personality and demeanor was not very appreciative toward us or the culprits who would not pay their share. Therefore, our family business project ended abruptly. Again, an unfortunate end to a job, and the feelings of helplessness to do more to change the outcome was my conclusion.

Drug Store Attendant

As I was approaching my teen years, I was hired by a local family-run drug store to be the out-front attendant while the pharmacist/owner serviced the customers with their prescriptions and other things associated with pharmacology. Meeting and greeting customers as they perused around the small store seemed like a natural fit for my growth as an employee and an individual. This position also produced my first thoughts of a career. Somewhat idolizing my boss, thoughts of becoming a pharmacist entered my mind, and following in his footsteps became a clear possibility at that time. However, as I would later find out in high school and college, the sciences were not my strength, and the thoughts of a pharmacy career went out the door.

Many theorists say that the mind has two sides; one for history, English, and the arts, and the other for math and science. I found out at an early age I'm much more inclined toward the artsy side then the geeky math and science side. No disrespect to the mathematicians and scientists of the world, but I much prefer creative reflection over the analytical and precise speculation. One type does not over rule the other; just simply "different strokes for different folks."

Young people may want try to figure out this differential in thinking or be guided toward their strengths by adult mentors in order to be placed on the right track when contemplating avenues to explore for future careers. Elementary schools need to emphasize the child's development in future aspirations and continue through the high school years to assist the young to become aware of life after graduation. Too many young people are confused and ill informed about the many possibilities that exist after whatever education level they find themselves.

As I focus back to my drug store attendant post, I believe my true motivation for entering into the pharmacy field was to somehow emulate the life of my boss and his family. I had my first "woman crush" for his wife. I used to dream of becoming part of their family and somehow replacing the husband and becoming the bread winner. Of course, all the rewards, which would include the affection of his wife, would then fall into place. Such devious thoughts, especially about the pharmacist, were surrounded by sexual curiosity that enters the minds of teenage boys. I did not realize at the time, I was maturing at a quicker pace than most of my childhood friends. I would later figure this out as time would pass and situations would occur where maturity would be a factor.

I eventually left my position at the drug store for a higher paying gig, but I will never forget those thoughts and dreams of impossible realities and fond memories.

Supermarket Worker/Cashier

My older cousin was a grocery manager in a large supermarket in our area. (It never hurts to have a connection or know someone who has a connection to a job that you want). He knew the manager of another large supermarket and with his influence; I landed my next position as a bag boy, cashier, and sometimes tractor-trailer product remover. The salary was much higher then my previous position, but with higher wages comes harder tasks and more difficult responsibilities.

The bag boy gig lasted a couple of weeks and simply consisted of helping the main cashiers put the groceries in paper bags for the customers to speed up the process. The pay was lower than for cashiers and along with the duties of the "bagger" came collecting the carts outside and bringing them in the store so more customers could reuse them and again leave them outside. This became a vicious cycle. I hated this assignment, and to this day, I feel a hint of sympathy for the poor guys that still have the unfortunate task of bringing in those stupid carts at Target and other large stores. However, because of my attention to task and willingness to be flexible, I was soon promoted to cashier.

I must emphasize that no matter what job you are performing, try to do the best that you can until the rewards come in. If your hard work and steadfast performance is not recognized after a period of time, then it's time to find another job. The worst thing you can do is to toil at a job you dislike and not perform appropriately. This will lead only to negative outcomes with the existing job and future opportunities.

During my time as a cashier, once again a "woman crush" entered my psyche, and dreams of connecting with this much older, but single, female became a nice distraction from the difficulties of the tasks and responsibilities of the job.

Before I continue, I must relate an incident that occurred early on during my time at the supermarket. My initial assignment, which was provided to me with the help of my cousin, was in a somewhat unsavory location in South Philly. (I later transferred to a much more desirable location after several months.) I would have to travel by bus from this location to my home, and at times, after dark.

One cold, wintry night, I was waiting for the bus at the corner where this store was located, when a man in a car approached me and asked if he could give me a lift. Since I saw him come out of the supermarket and get into his car, I figured he was a customer that I may have met in the store. Being somewhat naïve, and during a time when there was little news about predators, I somewhat reluctantly entered his car. Very quickly, his topic of conversation changed from very friendly to suggestive sexual encounters. A growing fear overwhelmed me, and at a red light, I simply opened the door and got out. I was in a very shady neighborhood, all alone and probably a mile or two from my home.

I walked extremely quickly, block by block, for about thirty minutes (which seemed more like hours) till I finally safely reached my home.

Upon entering my home, my mom immediately recognized my trepidation and asked what happened. Although I did not want to tell her any details, I swore I would never take a bus home from work again and would use my dad's car if I were going to continue to work at the supermarket. Having clearly witnessed my uneasiness, my family agreed that my dad's car would be available.

Although nothing serious happened to me that night, I had nightmares for several years about this incident. Nowadays, it is common for commuters or just people in general to be aware of their surroundings, and I wholeheartedly agree that they should be. However, imagine the horror of actually being a victim of one of these despicable child predators or even worse having a son or daughter violated by one of these wretched, detestable individuals. Be mindful that this could happen to anyone but don't let the horror overtake your trust in the majority of the "good" people in our world.

Returning to the supermarket, most of my time there will not be remembered in fond terms, but I performed my duties the best that I could. Despite the downsides, like accidentally turning over pallets of food products down the back of the building, having a bitchy supervisor who would not make an effort to help me with my weekly work schedule (eventually this inflexibility of scheduling led to my missing an important baseball game and my benching for our championship game which still lingers negatively to this day), and other misadventures too numerous to mention. It is amazing how a little power allows others to prey on the lesser types so they experience some sort of control, much like this catty supervisor at the supermarket. The positives were my wages paid for my years in college, and I had my first experience with union affiliation, which would become a much larger part of my future working life.

Roadie/Light Man

During my college days, some of my friends formed a musical group. Although I wanted to be part of the "group," my musical talent left much to be desired. In fact, basically I had no ability at all for anything involving music. However, the chance to travel some with the group for gigs, and possibly find some female attention that might come with the territory, appealed to me. I found my niche with the group by becoming a "roadie." I persuaded the guys in the group that I would be a great help for them in setting up and testing the sound and then packing the equipment back into our vehicles at the end of the gig. For this important job, I would receive a percentage of the amount they received for their performance.

The jobs were mostly at night and on the weekends, so I made myself available for most of the performances. For the most part, this little job was easy and enjoyable. During the time, the group played to mostly small bar audiences. I would circulate around the room to make sure the sound was even throughout the area while keeping my eye out for good-looking chicks. Not a bad deal for a young dude in his early twenties.

After a short period of time, the group expanded to include three "oldies" singers. Thoughts of making it big slowly entered our minds.

However, this development of popularity and appeal shortly became our demise. The group was taken over by a popular music manager in the area that wanted to form a band to perform "down the shore" in a club that he had contracted with. He promised everyone associated with the group, including myself, would be given important positions within his "empire," and we would all have the opportunity to move up in the music industry. However, his sights were really on the lead singer only and he couldn't care less about the rest of us. After a very short stint as a "light man" in his club, I was fired for not fully accepting his approach to his unacceptable demands.

Although, this venture was a brief encounter that ended negatively, I was happy to move on with my life and leave this unsavory situation.

Chapter Two

School Days

I GUESS I was one of the fortunate ones who realized what I initially wanted to do with my life in my sophomore year in high school. I was lucky to be placed in an English class with a wonderful teacher who presented the material with an interesting and insightful style. He was so influential to my inner self that I wanted to reproduce his teaching approach with my methods and eventually educate young people. I successfully completed my uneventful four years in college and obtained a teaching degree in order to maintain my "calling" of educating others.

As I stated, my college years were very unremarkable. I commuted to school using the local subway system in Philly but will always regret not attending a college away from home and becoming an on-campus student. I have witnessed my daughter living away from home at college and clearly recognized her growth in maturity and life experiences that I did not have the opportunity to develop at a similar age. Although my family could not afford to send me to a four-year institution away from home, I still could have attended a college with an on-campus lifestyle with student loans. However, I chose the safer and affordable local school.

After somewhat living my life through the eyes of my daughter and her college experiences, I still have some misgivings about the education decision I made "back in the day."

My advice to the youngsters contemplating the decision to stay local or live away from home when choosing a college is to clearly and completely review your choices and take everything into your decision making including; finances, family commitments, maturity, etc., in order to make a rational and levelheaded choice. If the opportunity presents itself, and the thought process is well constructed, then go for it!

Unfortunately, after graduating, the opportunity to teach in the high school environment (which was my choice) did not present itself immediately. I had to go through a period of time and several "jobs" before my education vocation was to be established.

Substitute Teacher

The movie/TV versions of "subs" in schools are not necessarily the reality of this position from my viewpoint. Although I longed for my own classroom and the financial rewards that came with a teaching position, my time as a substitute teacher was not painful. The classroom and the kids were the least of my worries. Uneven scheduling, low pay, taking sub opportunities only in "good" areas, and not moving forward with my life were my real issues. Granted, I was a bit untested in subject areas and student behavior; I still knew teaching would eventually be my salvation.

Insurance Salesman

This was my first introduction to an outside sales position. I wanted a job that was full time and would possibly produce the appropriate financial rewards that I so desired. After interviewing with two individuals that were very successful in the insurance industry, I chose to try this type of position. I hated it! I shadowed an individual who was doing extremely well and had joined the organization only a few months before I did. Of course, he made it look easy. We met with a few families who requested a brief meeting about their insurance needs. Some were very appreciative and accepting and others not so much. Either way, the agent I was shadowing used a heavy-handed, pushy approach that somehow worked. However, this was not my approach when attempting to sell my insurance policies. I guess I was too easygoing and not forceful enough to be a success in this demanding field.

Sales positions in general can be very rewarding both financially and in personal growth. However, you need to have that type A personality to sometimes "force the issue" when the sale may not be going in the right direction or to "close" the deal when it needs to be closed. It was very clear early in my personal development that I did not have that temperament that is essential for successful salespeople especially in the outside sales arena. I left the position without making a legitimate sale and the pursuit of some effective temporary replacement until I obtained my desired teaching position was still on my agenda.

Seasonal Department Store Worker

During my search for income during my pre-teaching years, I obtained a position with a major department store in Philly during the Christmas season as a sales person in the sporting goods section. The sporting goods area was on the third floor, and even during this busy time of year, the customer traffic was sparse.

Having cashier experience in previous employment, I easily adapted to the company's training and soon was given the responsibility to work alone in the department. The one word that would describe this experience was "boring." I found myself more interested in checking out the chicks (a theme of mine during this phase of my life) then actual work. However, the ability to be hired in different capacities, interviewing for various positions with a variety of individuals in charge of hiring, and placing myself in different environments, gave me experiences with many factors that would allow my development in preparing and obtaining many of my future positions.

Every chance you have to increase your knowledge and expand your horizons, no matter how common or routine the job may be, take the opportunity if it is presented to you. You never know what can develop or evolve from taking on even the simplest task. In this case, nothing developed or evolved for me, but nevertheless, I was involved in a different setting, although a humdrum one, and became more prepared for future endeavors.

Financial Advisor

This was another outside sales position but with possibly higher financial rewards and skilled training that could possibly result in a career. I guess I still hadn't figured out that I was not the type of individual that was going to be successful in a "sales" environment. I knew I enjoyed relating to people but was not confident enough to approach someone and try to sell them something–even with financial perks. However, the interview for this position went well, and I was told that ex-teachers and well-educated individuals were very successful in this type of field. I decided to give it a try, but within a few months or so, I once again realized outside sales was not my "thing."

Job Headhunter

Another sales job; what am I—a psycho? However, this position was inside sales! The job description was to cold call employers for job openings and try to get them to utilize the company's employee contacts to match their job needs. In addition, we were to interview perspective employees with all types of skills and attempt to counsel them to go on interviews that we provided for them. Of course, there were no shortage of potential employees, but the positions and the matching of perspective clients to available positions was very difficult. However, although the environment was very stressful, I was fortunate enough to work with an excellent sales person who was successful but also kind enough to take me under his "wing." He took the time to train me without interfering with his own duties and did so in an amiable and professional manner. He not only instructed me on the intricacies of the position but also provided me with an example of how one should train/supervise others, which would come into play during several of my future endeavors. In addition, the job counseling aspect of this position introduced me to a new and different avenue to eventually explore as a possible career.

Let me take a moment to further analyze the effectiveness, and in my opinion, correct approach to managing/supervising employees in any type of work environment. Too many times during my years in the work force, managers, supervisors, trainers, etc. take on an authoritative approach to assisting employees in their training or supervision and concentrated on their control and not the well being of the staff member. They feel they are in charge of the employee, and the worker needs to adapt to their style instead of the reverse. Many manager-types need to replace their ego with cordial, affirmative, and energetic applications to the tasks at hand, whether that is with instructing, educating, training, or simply supervising; similar to the young man that trained me at the job hunting agency.

Teachers also must adapt to students evolving into different types of complex personalities whose standards may be much different than in the past. Having stated the above about teachers, I must also emphasize that teaching young adults is a monumental task, especially during the current times and governmental restrictions that are major obstacles in the educational system. Teachers are today's heroes, and anyone that disparages the profession is simply a jackass! Much more on the teaching topic later.

Several times during my career, I was promoted within the same company. Some of these promotions were to positions where, at times, I would be supervising previous colleagues that were my equal in job status but were now my staff to supervise. I would always be cognizant of who I was and where I came from when supervision involved any type of staff member. However, I did not always find the same type of approach from many of the supervisors/managers that were directly above me in the organizational chart. Too often, several of my administrators/ directors could not shed their egos and took on their authority as a dictator instead of a leader.

Individuals who are given the responsibility to manage others should remember where they came from, why they are where they are, and how best to accomplish their undertaking with the same type of understanding and competence that they would like to have from someone supervising them. One of my favorite general comments that I have used when appropriate is "look in the mirror." That would be my assignment for all managers, supervisors, administrators, etc. If you could look at yourself in the mirror at the end of the day and feel satisfied about the way you treated an employee in any type of setting, or the way you trained or supervised someone, then you have produced a positive accomplishment.

Although I did not make much money or achieve any recognition during my time as a headhunter, I did learn some important aspects of the working life that I would utilize in several of my future job ventures.

Chapter Three

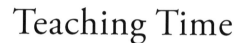

Teaching Time

Teacher

ALAS, MY CALLING of teaching in the high school environment was realized when I was given the opportunity to teach reading in the Philadelphia School District to selected students at a school only a few blocks from my parents' home. I was an English Education major in college, and fortunately, as part of the curriculum, I was obligated to take three reading courses, which gave me the requirements needed to qualify for the position. I was placed on a District list of teachers available for openings and was given the assignment of teaching reading at the local high school. Both my working and personal life grew in stature, and soon

I found myself "moving out" (almost six blocks from my childhood home—wow) and becoming an independent, financially secure, young adult. Life was good! However, as in the past and will be in the future, my overwhelmingly jubilant feelings of job security and positive developments would diminish over my almost-nine years of teaching in the Philadelphia Public School System.

For most of my teaching career, I enjoyed educating and cultivating the high school students assigned to my classroom over the years. I savored the memories of witnessing the maturity and development of the students into young adults ready to be productive citizens in the "outside" world.

My first assignment as a reading teacher quickly developed into a full-time English teacher instructing ninth through twelfth grade students from college-bound to slow learners. I slowly, but confidently, developed into a competent teacher and grew in experience, knowledge, and ability year by year. However, unfortunately, my beginning years of teaching placed me at the bottom of the "totem pole" with regards to seniority. Almost every year, near the end of the school year, I would be given "layoff" status, which inevitably would end the next year when I would be hired back, sometimes at the same school and sometimes at a different school within the Philly area. This constant unknown of where or whether my position would continue began to wear on my psyche, and thoughts of leaving the profession I had desired for years crept into my mind.

One particular year, I was reassigned to a middle school in Southwest Philly, in November, to a position that was occupied by substitute teachers from the beginning of the year. Imagine trying to take over a classroom of raging adolescents who had little or no discipline applied to them and were attempted to be instructed by several part-time instructors who probably were not educated in the subject at hand. One day, I came into the classroom and was greeted by two firemen who had just extinguished a fire in the drawer of my desk (one of my low points as a teacher). Needless to say, I used most of my sick time allotted during the next month or so until I was reassigned back to the high school that I began my teaching career and thanked God I was still alive (OK, I'm exaggerating but not really).

After my fourth year at my local high school, I was forced transferred, due to racial equality, to one of the oldest, and supposedly most undesirable, high schools in the school district. Of course, my trepidation over this transfer would cultivate my now conscious thought process of leaving teaching. However, I soon realized the school and its reputation was not justified, and even though the school was in one of the lowest economic areas of the city, the teaching faculty and administration excelled in their willingness to provide an excellent education to the eager student body. I, too, excelled in my teaching abilities at this school, and my attachment to some of these remarkable, deserving, and appreciative young students remains as some of my favorite memories of teaching to this day. I started rethinking my thoughts of leaving this noble profession and feeling more confident in my teaching skills. I seemed ready to develop a renewed commitment to guiding our youth.

However, I now began contemplating working inside the educational system but outside of the classroom. Therefore, I enrolled in a master's program at a local college to become a guidance counselor.

As what seemed to be a never-ending cycle in my working life, the positives soon evolved into negatives, and once again, my inclinations of leaving my passion for educating youth resurfaced due to some uncontrollable circumstances. First of all, the lack of mobility in the Philadelphia School District and scarcity of counseling positions placed an unfavorable slant on my desire to become a guidance counselor. However, the most adverse event that, unfortunately, happened while I was still teaching was a fifty-day worker strike that occurred before I left the teaching profession for good. This unfortunate experience placed a tremendous weight on my psyche. I had not yet been involved much with our professional union but supported their efforts to provide increases in salary and better working conditions. However, I did not have any idea what would take place during a strike and what my responsibilities were in supporting the union's purpose. The results of the strike were catastrophic in my view, even though the union and the school district finally settled on a small raise and some classroom concerns that were addressed as the final outcome.

While performing my duty of manning a picket line, I witnessed some of my colleagues, who were stanch union supporters, act horribly in some situations, especially involving those individuals that chose to cross the picket line. The name-calling, physical pushing/shoving, and verbal abuse was very far from professional to say the least, and I began to view some of my colleagues in a very different way. Professional educators who were previously viewed as comrades were now showing their real character by abusing not only the "scabs" but also the students and parents who may have had different perspectives toward striking. The whole scene was sickening to me, and even though I remained teaching for another two years, this fiasco convinced me to leave the "calling" that I thought would be my life's work since my high school years.

Thoughts of entering the "business" world became a reality when a friend of mine at that time, who would eventually become my loving wife, informed me of a temporary position available at the large corporation that she was employed. After some serious contemplation, I somewhat reluctantly resigned my teaching position with the school district, after almost nine years, to take a chance at a supplemental position with a large company in the computer industry. I distinctly remember my thoughts and anxiety of leaving a secure environment for an uncertain and completely contrasting work place. However, I knew that I did not want to remain in a classroom, and it seemed the alternative educational doors that I had explored were closed. Therefore, I made the decision to leave education and looked forward to the challenge of the new and different possibilities that the world and my life would present to me.

Just some thoughts here. Several times during my long (distinguished?) working life, I found myself having to make some contemplating decisions about leaving one position for another or just leaving for the unknown. I believe these decisions, some good, some not so much, developed my character and resolve to take on the challenges before me and fight harder to make them successful. I know I grew in maturity and self assurance by figuring out when life gives you a curve ball and knocks you on your ass, get back up ready to swing again. Too often I hear the "why me" approach to solving issues instead of taking on the confrontations, overcoming the fears of change, and hopefully, reaping the rewards of beating the odds and accomplishing positive results.

However, before I completely leave my teaching years, I must include the jobs I obtained during the summer time after the school year ended. This is traditionally an undertaking for many teachers during this time of the year since the salaries for educators in many areas of the country, are not conducive to just having the summers off without additional income. Some of these jobs were short in tenure but provided me with some great, and not so great, experiences, and at times, a lot of laughs.

Convenience Store Worker

A job I acquired during one of the summers during my teaching career was a worker in a local convenience store down the road where I now lived in a condo in South Jersey. I was hired due to my past super market experience, and although the work was tedious, the pay wasn't bad. I began by stocking shelves, unloading truck deliveries, and restocking freezer merchandise, which was a relief at times from the summer heat but became a hassle since I needed to bring extra clothes in case the freezer stuff needed adjustments.

An older couple owned and managed the store with the direction from corporate offices. They soon recognized my abilities and attention to detail and decided to promote me to assistant manager with a slightly higher pay raise. The responsibilities of this position far outweighed the increase in pay. I was immediately trained on the register, which came fairly easy to me due to my past experiences, and a few employees were now under my supervision.

In addition, I was given "closing" responsibilities, which were cleaning up after closing, counting money in the register, securing it in the safe, and locking the store for the night. For a twenty-three-year-old, these responsibilities were demanding. However, I decided to continue at this level, knowing in my mind that this was probably only a summer time assignment, although I did not relay this to management. (Sometimes holding back information for your benefit is the right thing to do in some working environments). They thought I would continue working after school began in a couple months. There was some thought on my part to continue beyond the summer, but I soon recognized that the work and duties were beyond my willingness to consider employment once the school year began. I also figured the owners realized I was a trustworthy individual, which would give them some relief from having the closing responsibilities. I understood everything that was occurring and chose to take on the conditions that were handed to me.

However, one night completely confirmed my mindset. After closing, and while cleaning the slicer machine, I sliced my hand on the very sharp blade of the machine. Blood splattered everywhere as I attempted to wrap my hand with a towel to somewhat curtail the stream of bright red blood. I somehow got in my car and drove to the emergency room (which fortunately was very close by) and received the appropriate amount of stitches that was required to close the wound. The incident, of course, caused some concern on my part, but the real anguish occurred when the management couple, after somewhat sympathizing with me about the injury, had the audacity to be a little upset that I didn't clean up the blood stains before I left so they would not have to clean it up the next day when opening the store. Since it was close to 1:00 am when I returned from the hospital, and fearing I had really damaged my hand, cleaning up had not entered my mind. This unfortunate situation happened near the end of the summer, so it was easy for me to quit immediately upon realizing the jackass management team cared more about their store than my well-being as one of their employees.

Several times in my career I have recognized that management sometimes will look past the employee's efforts or welfare to concentrate on the greater good of the company, corporation, school district, etc. that they serve in whatever capacity. Having served in several different types of management positions (as you will see as I continue to relay my employment in this book), I understand the need for management to sometimes separate their concern for the individual employee from the overall needs of the entity they serve. However, it is my opinion that this separation should only occur when all else has been scrutinized and the only true result is to favor the organization and overlook the employee's needs. Too often, management/administration take on the realization that the organization always comes first, and the employee is a distant second. As you will read in the following chapters, I was able to distinguish that fine line as a manager and understood the main focus should be for the individuals that make up the backbone of the company/corporation and not the managers whose authority sometimes over rules their consciousness.

Summer Camp Counselor

One of my most pleasant job memories was the one summer I spent as a camp counselor in South Philly. The "counselor" description in the job title was definitely not the essence of the position. For the most part, it was allowing the middle school aged kids to have fun while on summer break from school. The counselor was mainly responsible for counting the kids as they got on the bus in the morning and counting them again as they got back on the bus at the end of the day's activity to make sure everyone returned home safely. The counselors would gather together, and with one eye on the kids, we would discuss such diverse subjects as "who was going out with who" and other such matters that would enter the minds of twenty-something-year-old young adults. We would play games with the kids but would always fixate on the female/male relationships that were developing on a daily basis. Love was truly "in the air."

I, too, became infatuated with a young female counselor that I thought connected with me on several levels. Although I knew she had a boyfriend, our daily interactions brought on palpitations in my heart. We would laugh and kid each other like secret lovers with most of the reflection in my mind only. This one-way attraction happened several times in my love life until I finally met my lovely wife of thirty plus years. Even though we are now truly soul mates, it still took her awhile before she actually realized our connection, and we got hitched. At the camp, I knew there was an attraction on both sides, but I also knew I was out-matched by her college basketball playing boyfriend. Such is the outcome of many young adults dealing with finding a meaningful relationship.

Although the times and events with this position are fondly remembered, there were some disturbing situations that now, when I think back, I probably should have paid more attention to. There were a few of the hundred or so kids who were not treated appropriately. The other kids basically bullied them. I remembered feeling sorry for them and attempted to stop the bad behavior of some of the other kids, but not paying close enough attention to their actions and reactions of the victims.

Some of the mistreated kids adapted and stayed together to ward off the bullies. However, one particular youngster was treated poorly simply because he looked different and was a little slower than the others. He would be very defiant and nasty to everyone whenever he felt threatened which I now realize was his defense mechanism. He was tough to get to know and like, but he still deserved a better fate. I found myself, at first, trying to resolve issues with him and others, but when his attitude would be disrespectful, I backed off. In addition, he was not part of my assigned kids, so I left decisions up to his counselors. He got through the summer and seemed to have some good times, but the last day, his mom was furious at his counselors because he broke his glasses in a scuffle with some kids. I'm sure he would not have remembered that summer in a warm hearted way.

There is so much more attention now focused on bullying in the schools, which is a tremendous improvement from years past. Teachers and parents need to be very cognizant of the student interactions, especially with middle school kids where many of the bullying behavior begins and festers. Parents must be more aware of their children's demeanor, and any changes in a negative manner should be investigated and resolved. Once the child enters the high school environment, it may be too late to have parent involvement make a difference. Many schools now employ student assistance counselors who are professionally trained to focus on student behavior, especially dealing with bullying, harassment, and intimidation.

Hopefully, parents and students will take advantage of the counseling provided by schools and the staff responsible for this undertaking.

School Maintenance Worker

Many of my working summers were spent "down the shore" in Wildwood, New Jersey, to be specific. My first and briefest summer employment was at the local high school as a maintenance worker. I answered an ad in the local newspaper for this position because I needed and wanted some type of job so I could afford my lavish lifestyle at the shore (Ha!). From the minute I walked into the place to the minute I left (an eight hour shift, three days a week) I worked like a dog. There was always a job to do, according to my supervisor, an elderly gentleman, who always seemed to be sitting down while everyone else worked. I cleaned, painted, and scrubbed everything in sight. I moved furniture and desks from one side of the building to another and every other task that was needed in the school building. The final straw came when I was assigned to clean the bathrooms, which had not been cleaned since the kids left in June. The result was a week (three days) of these chores, and off I went. Luckily, a friend of mine let me know that there was an opening in a downtown hotel. Thank heavens my sentence as a maintenance worker had a short life, and I would soon find out the hotel gig would become a very pleasant experience and last for several summers.

Parking Lot Attendant

My buddy who let me know about the opening was working for the hotel as a parking lot attendant. The lot was attached to the back of the hotel and was rented per car for customers who wanted to visit the boardwalk that was just a short walk from the hotel. The job was to be one of these parking attendants, and the only necessity needed was a valid drivers license. The fact that my buddy put in a good word for me was also a small factor in my hiring, but I believe anyone with a pulse would have been hired since management needed someone desperately to fill a shift for this very active parking facility. However, remember as I stated previously, it never hurts to know someone or have some connection in order to secure employment of any kind.

I found myself in a very enjoyable situation, and the duties of jockeying the cars from one spot to another to accommodate the influx of autos waiting their turn to visit the hot spots on the boardwalk was, for the most part, painless. I soon felt that I had acquired the ability to move quickly from one car to another, and with an appropriate amount of speed, placed each vehicle in an assigned spot. In addition, when the customers would return from their destinations, I would collect their keys and bring their car to them quickly, which at times, solicited a nice monetary tip. All was well with the job and the social interactions, which developed for this single guy and the female populace.

However, as usual, there always were interruptions in my jobs, and the parking attendant stint was no exception. One very busy night, I got into an older model vehicle, which I found out later needed full pressure on the brakes in order to come to a full stop. Well, as I'm sure you can figure out, I maneuvered this vehicle in back of another car, and with my newfound expertise of driving faster then I should, rammed into the car in front and damaged its rear end. In addition, the force of the hit moved the car in front over the barrier and into the wall of the hotel so both the front and back of the car were damaged. As I reluctantly got out of the car, and upon hearing the shouts of my supervisor, I couldn't believe that out of the two hundred or so cars in the lot, I hit my friend's brand new Mercury Cougar. What were the friggin' chances?

My supervisor, who was an older gentleman, relieved my anxiety a little by assuring me that the damage was actually not too extensive, and the hotel's insurance would fully cover the costs. However, I still had the regrettable task of telling my friend that, of all the cars in the lot, I inexplicably damaged his new car. By the way, this particular friend was going through some personal issues and tried solving them by drinking and indulging in other substances. I found him in a local club sitting at a bar getting "shwasted." Luckily for me, with the substances he digested, I don't believe he totally understood the magnitude of my encounter with his car, and therefore, lessened the explanation I needed to give him.

The next day when he was sober, I drove him to the auto shop that was repairing his precious Cougar and reassured him that everything would be paid for, and his vehicle would be up and ready to cruise in a short period of time. In the meantime, as somewhat of a repayment, I drove him anywhere and everywhere he wanted to go until his car was fully repaired.

Fortunately for me, I had performed my duties prior to this unfortunate accident with good work habits, getting to work on time, and being an overall good guy. These attributes not only saved my job, but I had become a favorite son of the Italian family that owned the hotel, the parking lot, an attached liquor store, a cocktail lounge (also on the premises), and a small bar in another section of the town. It was like being back in South Philly with the owners named Tony, Angelo, Rita, and Mary and the other Italian goombas! They would continue to hire me in different capacities each summer for the next several years, and I relished in a supportive, family-like atmosphere that allowed me to grow socially, emotionally, and in self-assurance.

Lifeguard

Ok, it was really called "pool boy," but to anyone asking, I was the Lifeguard at the hotel pool. After my stint as a parking lot attendant, the management (now referred to as my "peeps") chose to elevate me to this important position. My duties consisted of cleaning the sides of the pool early in the day before any of the hotel occupants would arrive, insuring the pool mechanics were in proper order, and basically sitting under an umbrella watching scantily attired females jump in and out of the pool. Of course, there were all types of male and female shapes entering the pool area, but my eyes zoomed in on the curvaceous females.

My life saving training consisted of being able to swim the length of the medium-sized pool that started at three feet at one end and ended at eight feet at the other. Luckily, there were no incidents of any kind during my summer at the pool that required any lifeguard skills, but unfortunately, this would change at a later date. I thoroughly enjoyed this particular summer but again continued to have the work ethic that allowed me to appreciate my job but also adhere to the responsibilities that my employers (pseudo family) had given me. This work integrity would remain as a staple throughout my varied career and should be a goal to attain by everyone, no matter what position you acquire.

Hotel Front Desk Attendant

The following summer after lifeguarding (or whatever), I was promoted to the hotel's front desk as a valued customer greeter and securer of hotel rooms for the guests. My hours for this position varied, and at times, I would come in very early. At other times, I would be assigned to the night shift that ended at 10:00 pm. My personality was a natural for this position, and I worked with a couple of females that were part of the hotel family who treated me with respect and kindness. I enjoyed this position immensely and became very socially active, especially at the hotel's cocktail lounge, which was my hangout after my night shift. I continued to be delighted to work in this supportive environment.

However, a deplorable incident happened during this time that I will remember for the rest of my life. While I was working at the front desk during the day shift, some commotion was heard at the pool area, and I was instructed to go out and see what was going on. As I moved closer to the pool area, I realized that the guys working at the pool that day were attempting to remove an unconscious individual from the water and place him at the edge of the pool. Screams of anguish and verbal pleas of prayers to God were heard as several individuals tried to revive the young male that was lying motionless. Shortly, an ambulance with paramedics arrived, and they too attempted resuscitation but to no avail. The male swimmer had died from drowning.

It so happened that this particular day was very bright and sunny and the brightness made it impossible to see anything but the top of the water in the pool. Evidently, the young man must have dove into the pool, somehow hit his head, and sunk to the bottom. One of the pool workers saw a shadow at the bottom of the pool when he was swimming and went down to investigate. He found the body and immediately brought him to the surface, but it was too late.

I found out later, that the young man who expired was on his honeymoon with his extended family and that made the horrifying incident that more dreadful. I remember feeling immediately nauseated while witnessing this wretched episode and felt that way for several days after the incident. This disastrous occurrence has remained with me as one of the most distressing experiences of my life.

I wonder, at times, why God allows such atrocities to happen which will shake one's faith. However, although I am not the most "religious" person, I do trust in the Higher Power and will continue to believe in God and pray that nothing remotely as bad as this, or any other tragic situation, happens to me or any of my family, friends, and loved ones. Sorry to end this particular positive working experience with this unfortunate story, but sometimes life will produce stark realities to even the most pleasant memories.

Liquor Store Manager

Getting back to more cheerful news, the next summer I was again promoted (I guess) to the important position of the person in charge of the family owned liquor store and the responsibilities that were part of the job. I was to supervise one other worker that would share the hours of operation with me. I would be responsible for the money that was collected for the purchase of the booze and other non-alcoholic products sold at the store. The duties also included making sure enough products were displayed on the shelves and ordering merchandise from suppliers when needed. The store was small so it was not too much to handle for a young dude like myself. Again, I was treated well, both financially and respectfully, by my adopted family, and the position was a pleasure to participate in.

My first thoughts of entrepreneurial endeavors entered my mind at this time and would come to fruition much later in my life. Remember, during these summer employment positions, I was teaching, and my mindset was still centered on education. Thoughts of changing careers were limited to far in the future, which eventually became reality. One delightful memory I recall during my time at the liquor store was at the end of each night's shift, which was at 9:00 pm, the band next door at the cocktail lounge would begin their set with Van Morrison's tune "Moondance." (To this day, every time I hear that song, I get good vibes). Of course, that tune singled the end of my work shift and the beginning of my social time at my nightly hang out right next door, the Midtown Lounge.

Bartender

Moving right along in my summer employment adventures, I was positioned by my hotel family at the cozy bar they owned that was not part of the main facility. This establishment was in the non-tourist side of town and inhabited by mostly the locals that were permanent residents of this shore town. Not having any bartending experience, I was trained by the head bartender to basically pour glasses of beer from the kegs for the customers making sure there was a "head of foam" at the top of the glass and becoming familiar with the liquor bottles that were available to customers for mostly shots. Yes, this was a shot and beer bar!

I started working the day shifts, which began at 9:00 am and ended at 5:00 PM. Therefore, mixed drinks were an oddity with an occasional 7 and 7 thrown in. I would witness the same group of characters that came in at 9:00 am when the doors opened have a sandwich from the kitchen for lunch go home around 4:00 pm, only to return with a change of clothes and more orders of fifteen cent glasses of beer. (I found this out after working the later shifts after several weeks of training.) How these individuals that apparently didn't work survived this routine day in and day out was mind-boggling.

During the nighttime, especially weekends, the bar would actually become a bustling, lively, entertaining place with cheerful songs and spirited debates. Once in awhile, an overly polluted individual or two would have to be escorted out of the premises, and the police would get involved, but this did not happen very often. For the most part, the day crowd, although depressing, would be calm and somewhat happy, and the night group would consist of the regulars with different clothes and the friends and relatives of the regulars. I began to become the typical listening bartender who would be friendly but realize that if the customer wanted to talk, just let him and agree to what they related.

My bartending time (which was my last year of summer employment with my hotel family) was enjoyable for the most part until I received the news from my management family that I was going to be "moving up" to the big time cocktail lounge. At first, I was very excited about this opportunity, even though it was occurring at the end of the summer and would only be for a one-night audition. One of the bartenders at the lounge had to leave before the Labor Day weekend, and that Sunday I was to "step it up" and perform the duties of a "real" bartender. The money for that one night, including tips, would exceed what I made for a week at the neighborhood bar.

However, my excitement would turn to apprehension when I realized I would have to be given a crash course on preparing drinks that

I may have heard about but never served. The other friendly and experienced bartenders assured me that they would help me. I was given a "cheat sheet" to assist me if I received a drink order that I was unfamiliar with, or worse, never heard of.

That night I decided to indulge in a foreign substance to help me calm down. (OK, I smoked a joint! It was the seventies.) What a mistake! Not only did the "extra curricular stuff" not calm me down, but it worked in the opposite direction and made me a paranoid wreck. The place was rocking, and the noise was deafening. Not only was it difficult to hear, but also, soon after the customer would order a drink, I would turn around and forget what they just ordered and would have to ask several times before it finally clicked in. In addition, the bar had a lip on the edge, and inevitably, I would place the drink on the lip and almost spill every drink I served. I remember shouting to myself to "GET STRAIGHT" and pounding my foot on the floor to bring me to my senses. After several hours in fear of imploding, the night finally came to an end around 2:00 am. I had survived the ordeal, and no one really noticed that I was an incompetent fool high on weed for most of the time. Although this episode remains as a hilarious story that I have related many times to my friends, it was a nightmare while it happened.

So ends my time in the summer winds down the shore and the jobs I secured. Although there were many good times, there were also some upsetting situations and occurrences. However, I grew as an individual and developed a self-assurance that I previously lacked. Some of the jobs were menial; some involved maturity and responsibility, but I learned to perform well in many types of environments and to take the experiences, both good and bad, as the beginning stages of my evolution into a self-confident, self-assured adult while still looking for that puzzling occupational career that would satisfy my true goal of self-actualization. This goal would become a life long search that would be a constant challenge.

Working is a large part of one's life. Try to find a working environment that is pleasing to your mindset and fits your desire to accomplish something meaningful in your life. Not everyone can find this elusive life enhancing opportunity, but attempting it is much better than accepting the unwanted reality. Educate yourself, become self-reliant, experience the positives and the negatives, introduce yourself to new and different training, attempt diverse ideas, develop goals, and don't lose site of them. All of the above, and then some, will allow you to grow as an individual and maybe pass on your experiences to others. I have had a lifetime of ups and downs, as you will further read. I have some regrets and many rewards, but I can honestly relay that I always attempted to "be the best I can be."

Chapter Four

All Over The Place

Supplemental Computer Dispatch Employee

To REVIEW MY working life history at this point, despite much apprehension, I had made the decision to leave the teaching field that I initially contemplated as my career choice and life-long ambition. A tremendous challenge was before me. My only extended experience was in the academic area, and my resumé showed as much. Therefore, I had to rely on friends to provide opportunities that would allow me to change careers and enter the "business" world. As I mentioned, my close friend and future wife worked for many years with a large, well-known computer company and enjoyed working at the large corporation. She would also relate how cool it was to work in the big city (Philly) and the social interactions that came with the territory.

I must comment here that I would highly recommend NOT leaving one position without having another in place. I choose this route during this time. However, there were situations in my career that I left a position without any knowledge of what my next step in the employment process would be. But again, it is much easier to have a job ready before leaving another position unless your well-being is affected so much that getting out is your only option.

The position available at this large corporation for someone without much computer or business experience was a six-month supplemental dispatch position that I interviewed for and was hired prior to leaving my teaching position. Initially, as happened in previous stages in my life, joyous excitement entered my being, feeling that with this opportunity, I would prove my abilities to adapt to different kinds of tasks, and that my business career would "take off" from there. This position was going to be my "stepping stone" to a full-time position, and become an easy transition from the teaching field.

Once again, soon after my training stint, things beyond my control began to unravel, and I spiraled downward in confidence and spirit. The administrator assigned to me was new to his position and seemed to have less knowledge about the particulars of the dispatching process then I did as a new employee. This manager was somehow promoted to the position without the proper training in supervision and/or relevance to the positions he was supervising.

I am amazed how companies, corporations, school districts, etc., promote certain individuals. I have witnessed these atrocities several times in my career and marvel at the ineptitude and lack of ability of some of these characters that are promoted. I am bewildered at times with how an administration can make such drastic mistakes. At times, I believe certain people get promoted simply because the entity they are working for can't figure out what to do with them, since firing someone becomes difficult with equality, unions, and seniority. This situation was my first witness to several of these promotion inequities. By the way, I don't enjoy disparaging this particular individual, but in addition to his incompetency, he would douse himself with cologne before he came in to work, and it would remain throughout the work area for hours whenever he came out of his office, which was rare. I would look for his help in dealing with this stressful situation but received only senseless suggestions or minimal instruction simply because he was so uninformed about his job and the responsibilities of a supervisor.

This position consisted of having a phone attached to my ear to receive the multitude of calls from co-workers, sales reps, area supervisors, and other pertinent personnel. Sales reps would want to know where and when the product they ordered for their customers would be delivered along with why any time discrepancies occurred with the dispatching process, so they would be paid as quickly as possible. The area supervisors, feeling pressure from their management team, wanted everything to run as smoothly and accurately as possible and did not want to hear when the process was not moving appropriately enough. They did not want to take on the responsibility of figuring out why. This was supposed to be the job of the dispatcher. I worked with a team of three other dispatchers, all permanent employees, one of which was attempting to train me while she was performing her duties. Needless to say, there were some issues with the entire dispatching process and as the "rookie/new guy," I would be blamed for the mistakes even if I had not caused them. The environment became extremely stressful, and I felt failure for the first time.

After a month or so, I actually thought things had settled down and that I was doing better in handling the adversity. When I was called into the manager's office, I thought he was going to complement me for turning things around. However, to my ultimate despair, he told me I was fired and that the end of the week would be my last day. I was devastated. I had left a secure and viable teaching position for this temporary spot that I was now being fired from. Fear and embarrassment entered my world.

That evening, I had to tell my family who were not all on board with my decision to leave teaching that I had failed miserably. Not only I was fired, but also, what was next? Who would hire someone without experience and without a job at hand? I was at one of the lowest periods of my life. My self-confidence was at an all time low.

Most people that get fired from a position, whether it's their fault or not, have some anxiety about the unknown. Getting past self-pity and taking on the challenge is the right course of action even though, depending on the circumstances, it may be quite difficult to take this approach. I dreaded going in the next day and facing something I had never dealt with before.

Believe it or not, that very next day, I was told by this incompetent manager that one of the area supervisors had interceded for me and basically convinced upper management that there were many other factors involved that caused problems with the dispatching process and that I should not be held responsible. I was rehired, and my job would be secure for the six-month duration. I later found out that this company had no intention of promoting any of the supplemental employees to full-time status and that they conceived these positions as a way to save money by not hiring permanent employees therefore reducing payroll and medical expenses.

Nevertheless, I was relieved to say the least and felt a glint of inner success with this reprieve. Not only had I overcome this negative outcome, even though my firing was only for a day, I began to gain confidence in my abilities. I also discovered a newfound appreciation from my co-workers and supervisors for having someone who had never personally met me stand up to management and confirm what I knew was a wrongdoing and convert it into a positive result.

From that day on, everything turned in a positive direction, and my work performance became a source of inner pride. I received a written commendation from the area supervisor that saved my job, and I shortly became "one of the boys" with the permanent employees. I enjoyed the active social interaction that was one of the perks that I desired when entering this atmosphere. I even wrote a couple of humorous articles for the in-office newsletter, which were received well by co-workers and management. I had witnessed adversity and felt that I could handle whatever comes next, even though outside influences assisted in my succeeding in this endeavor.

However, no matter how well I performed or assimilated into the working environment, I was still a supplemental and had no chance to remain as a full-time employee. All the supplemental staff that were hired during my tenure were given cursory interviews, not knowing at the time that the company had no intentions of hiring any of us. The company later discontinued this practice when someone brought a lawsuit against them.

The final result after the computer position ended was a time that I had to deal with that did not have any definite direction. I had to figure out what was my next move. Luckily, I did receive unemployment compensation after my departure and during that time made plans to develop a strategy that included training and cultivating. I developed a thought process to take on the challenge of finding employment that would encourage my growth as a self-assured individual.

Unemployment compensation is a way of regrouping and rethinking without the strain of acquiring income. In my opinion, it is a necessity for the middle-to lower-class in order to adjust to negative employment outcomes, and if used wisely and properly, should result in the appropriate chance to educate and train oneself for other opportunities while not starving.

Each and every obstacle in one's working life should empower the individual to take on the challenge, develop the new opportunities, and strive to succeed. I have taken on this approach with every hurdle thrown my way in every type of situation in my life, work or non-work related. As you will witness in reading this book, for whatever reason, I have and will encounter several other somewhat disastrous episodes in my working life. I had to overcome negative events with strong and concise effort and unrelenting determination. I was convinced that I would conquer the challenges and remain steadfast in my confidence in "who I am" and what I can accomplish.

Radio Producer

Say what? How the heck did I get into the entertainment business? Well, as I mentioned previously, unemployment compensation, if used appropriately, can result in opportunity for training and/or possibly changing careers. After the end of the supplemental position, I was fortunately provided with unemployment compensation in order to help attempt to find another working environment.

During this time, I decided to enter a training institute that advertised opportunities in the radio/TV industry that would be available to the graduates of their program. Prior to enrolling into this establishment, I researched the company and found some promising results for several of their past students. Make sure you take the effort to research, analyze, and inquire about any training program before taking the leap forward and enrolling, especially if the program promises employment.

After a few months of training with radio station equipment and performing some on-air short excerpts for a rarely listened radio station, I put together a resumé that would accentuate my new established training and the fact that I minored in communications at Temple University. I sent out numerous resumés to several local TV and radio stations with the intent on possibly finding an entry-level position in the industry. To my amazement, I was contacted by a major radio station in the Philly market to come in and interview for a position as a producer. Of course, I was excited and enthused, and thoughts of entering the communications arena as a career possibility was a dream that now entered my thoughts. However, first I had to prove at an interview that I was worthy of this opportunity.

I went into the interview with some apprehension but confident that I could get the job. Having interviewed many other times in different venues, I began gaining more assurance in my abilities to adapt to various situations and started approaching interviews in a positive manner, rather than dreading the process. This became a strong attribute and confidence building skill for several of my future interviewing opportunities. I was interviewed by the station manager and the head producer and was thrilled to be hired. The salary, however, was not great, but the possibility of future growth in the industry was a real "turn on."

After training for a week or so, I began working as a behind the scenes producer for various talk show hosts who would shed their wisdom to the audience and invite whomever to call in live and agree or debate their positions on the topic at hand. My responsibilities were to screen the callers and place them on air when their turn came up. In addition, I would remind the host for commercial breaks and make sure he or she was ready to return to live feed once the commercials ended.

The process was hectic at times but interesting and entertaining. Some hosts were very gracious and thanked me for my efforts on air and also after their shift on their way out. However, there was one egomaniac that thought he was God's gift and treated everyone at the station with disdain. Of course as the "rookie" at the station, he would berate my performance, and instead of encouraging me like other personalities did, he would blame me for anything that did not go in a positive direction with the callers. At this time, especially after going through some past difficult situations in my working life, I now had the ability to take on the challenge from this a-hole and go directly at him with the tenacity of a seasoned veteran. Many of the staffers appreciated my ability to stand firmly to my resolve and congratulated me after the ego-tist realized that his rants would not affect me. He eventually became a much more friendly and accepting individual toward others and myself at the station after several of our verbal battles.

I relate this little tidbit to reemphasize that I obtained my resolve to "fight my battles" after several past indiscretions and learned from these experiences. This determination would not have developed if I did not go through some rough times in my past. Therefore, I again emphasize that when circumstances go south, grasp the experience and learn from it. You will be better prepared for any further situations that may not go your way and take on these "bumps in the road" as challenges to succeed.

Although I remained in this position for over a year, I could not afford the limited income while waiting for a promotional opportunity to come my way.

Sometimes wishing for results doesn't always become reality and "you have to do what you have to do" in order to survive. I decided to take on a position with a non-profit organization (which became my next avenue of employment for many years) during the week daytime hours and continued to work on the weekends at the station during the overnight hours. Yes, I was working seven days a week, and my social life was basically non-existent. However, I remained at the radio station for a time while working two jobs because I continued to believe that my "ship" would come in. That never happened but it was fun while it lasted.

During these overnight shifts, some interesting and somewhat bi-zarre happenings occurred. I was the producer of a Saturday night show called "Desperate and Dateless." (How about that title for a program!)

My duties were to interview the perspective candidates prior to going on air and match them up with other males or females that would be willing to go on a date with them. The host would then suggest that the participants call back in a week or so to let the listeners hear how things went with the date. For the most part, these individuals that called in were hilarious. Every now and then a dating set-up would actually work out for the couple, and they would relate their continuing relationship in future weeks on the show.

While fielding these calls for dates, I had my first and only experience with "phone sex" which was interesting but not my "thang"! I later met the female of this experience at a radio event but nothing further developed.

In addition, the main host infrequently would not be available for the program due to sickness or some other reason, and I would be his back up. This was my first, and only, real on-air action. Several people at the station had informed me that I have a voice for the radio. This opportunity, even for a whimsical trial period on "Desperate and Dateless," gave me a hint of what could be in store if the opportunity presented itself. I gave a year of my life to attempt to advance in this industry, but my chance at stardom was only for a moment.

This particular radio station still exists in the big time Philly market but changed to an all-sports format after I left. I often think if I had remained and somehow carved out a living during my time at the radio station that I would have related much better to a sports station rather than to a topical call in station. Maybe that illusive opportunity in the entertainment arena that I was hoping for would have come my way.

Chapter Five

The Non-Profit Experience

Public Relations Assistant

As I STATED previously, I was still working at the radio station on the weekends when I decided to apply for a position in public relations with a non-profit organization. I actually found the description of the position in the Want Ads in the paper. That's how we found some jobs "back in the day." I put together a resumé that accentuated my radio experience and my communications background. I was called in for an interview with an interesting individual that was somewhat giddy during our meeting but knowledgeable in the public relations area. She was impressed with my radio position and hired me on the spot. My salary would be $4.25 an hour, which at that time was minimum wage. In addition, I would be getting full medical benefits, which was a perk with non-profit organizations. This low salary was one of the reasons I was working seven days a week along with the hope that one or the other of my positions would lead to upward growth and job security.

The public relations position was to assist the director (the director and myself would comprise the entire department) in promoting the positive accomplishments of the organization and the future direction, which would continue its mission of rehabilitating the mentally and physically handicapped. I would later find out that the director of the department was an ex-nun who would not hide the fact that she was now a sexually active female. Thankfully, I did not stay in this position for an extended period of time, so there was no chance of any "hanky panky" within the department. However, several other male employees made known their encounters with this woman. I only mentioned this to relate the possibilities of having a supervisor that may be different or unusual. Although this person was someone I would never have imagined would be my boss, she was still a very competent individual and I respected her for her abilities as they related to the job. I did not let any outside influences undermine my efforts toward the tasks that she required of me.

One of my first assignments was to call retail companies and request clothing, small appliances, and other miscellaneous items to be donated to our organization for resale in the agency's thrift stores. However, the emphasis would be on what was referred to as "new goods" which were items that were not yet used by the public and may be characterized as excess inventory or slightly damaged unsold goods that were still sale-able. These items were especially good sellers in the thrift stores, and the store managers were continuously requesting "new goods" to enhance the profits of their respective stores.

A budget was allocated to the sales director to purchase "new goods," but the money was always in short supply and did not equal to a year round addition to the thrift store's inventory. Previously, this project was not a priority and basically had no direction. I decided to dive into this activity in order to solidify my hiring and to exhibit my abilities. I spent a certain amount of hours each day calling on these companies and kept copious notes of when and how to generate these precious "new goods" items. I soon found out that part of the reason that this project was not successful in the past was because there were stipulations and time frames by the retail companies that had to be adhered to in order for the goods to be donated.

Some of these stipulations would involve calling back at different seasons of the year, especially for clothing outlets, or within the next week or so when they were ready to donate.

Follow-up was an important factor. I was able to ensure the companies' arrangements would be handled properly by communicating with the transportation department of our organization to establish a working relationship with the retail companies. Within a short period of time, the "new goods" flowed into our agency, and word spread that the guy in public relations was making a difference. There was a direct positive result by the thrift stores who generated the income that was used for the rehabilitation efforts of the organization.

I remained in this position for only about six months but presented a difference in the job's description, how to proceed with future assistants, and essentially created the important need for the position. I left this job due to a promotional opportunity within the organization. I believe this promotion was granted because of my efforts in the public relations department position. I reiterate, once again, that no matter how low level or menial your job may be, do your best, and you will be noticed and appreciated or if not, find another job. With this promotion and opportunity of growth within this organization, I somewhat reluctantly left my radio gig and seven days a week routine for an established five day a week, salaried position.

Counseling Supervisor

Within this non-profit organization was a counseling component that assisted the mentally and physically handicapped individuals in a sheltered workshop that worked at the agency's corporate building. The counselors also helped the job-ready candidates to find employment in the agency's thrift stores and outside the sheltered environment. The handicapped individuals would range from drug and alcohol dependent to wheelchair bound adults who would have difficulty finding a "regular" job on their own. The counselors would have a varying caseload. Their jobs were to counsel and improve the self-confidence of the sheltered members in order to apply and be hired by companies in the area. The agency would offer tax credits to places of employment that would take on the handicapped as regular workers. One of the four counselors would have the responsibility to go out and find perspective employers and job openings.

The counseling department had an opening for a position as a supervisor to coordinate the counselors' activities and responsibilities and to ensure that they were performing their jobs appropriately. At this juncture of my working life, I had completed several courses in acquiring a master's degree in counseling that began when I was still in education. All of the other counselors working at the facility had undergraduate degrees or a few years of college study. I put together a resumé that was beginning to grow in flexibility that enhanced my teaching degree and my partially completed master's degree. I now had accumulated a mixture of jobs that I could rearrange to emphasize the area of employment that I wanted to apply to. In this case, I used my educational experience and my previous success in my other position within the organization to secure an interview with the director of the rehabilitation department.

In addition, during my time in public relations, I intentionally presented a friendly demeanor to whomever I came in contact with within the agency. This was not at all difficult for me since my personality tends to be naturally sociable and friendly. During this process, I became particularly friendly with the director that granted me the interview for the counseling supervisor position and felt confident when I sat down with her for the interview.

Using your positive personality to connect with those within your employment environment, whether to attempt to move "up the ladder" or simply to present yourself as a confident individual, is clearly a way to integrate into your new surroundings. It may also encourage management to view you as a potential employee for promotional opportunities. However, be yourself, and do not pretend to be friendly if it is against your nature. Management will quickly recognize "pretenders."

Find an attribute in your personality that will underscore positive reactions from others, and use this to the best of your ability.

The interview was lengthy, and although I knew I had given my best, I was informed by the director that she would be continuing to interview others for the position. During the interview, I had to "sell myself" since this was a new and different type of employment, and although counseling was a clear interest; I did not possess any direct counseling or supervisory experience. I pursued this opportunity because I was confident in my abilities even though the work experience was not there. My self-assurance was growing and taking on challenges was my norm, and I would continue to develop my self-confidence during my future employment. After about a week, I was granted a second interview with the director and the head of the organization, the executive director. Although I was a little nervous, since this was my first time at a second interview, I presented myself as an individual that was very capable and would continue to develop a successful approach to this supervisory position. Before the interview ended, I was offered the position and was thrilled that my self-assuredness secured this desirable opportunity for me.

Not all challenges will end up in a positive manner. If you do not succeed initially, continue to accept the possibility of accomplishments and take the approach that "nothing is impossible" unless you don't try!

I was now in my first supervisory capacity in a counseling area and was excited about fulfilling my goals to be a successful manager and grow with the position. I reentered the master's program in a local college, and within a short period of time, completed my degree. I now possessed a graduate degree in a discipline that I had sincere interest in pursuing.

Initially, I had to overcome the somewhat awkward development of supervising employees that were previously my co-workers. One of the counselors had a negative attitude, feeling that he should have been promoted to the position instead of myself. I sat down with this employee, and in a tone that I didn't realize I possessed, explained to him that I appreciated his concerns but that I expected him to continue working effectively and completing his responsibilities to the handicapped individuals that he counseled. He left my office on friendly terms but let it be known that he was going to apply for positions elsewhere and would let me know when he found an appropriate position for his skills and experience. This occurrence was my first encounter with an employee that was not "on board" with my philosophy and certainly would not be my last as a supervisor/manager. Within a few weeks, this individual left the agency, and I congratulated him on his new position and appreciated his honesty in relating his concerns. His job with our agency mostly consisted of finding jobs for our handicapped clients, which was an important, and very active, position within the agency.

My next duty was to find a replacement for this open position. I placed an ad in the newspaper and immediately received several resumés that fit the description of the position and called in several candidates to interview. After narrowing the search to two individuals, the interviewing process continued with the director, and a decision was mutually agreed upon. The individual selected was a success during my tenure as his supervisor.

The above tale brings to light my development in not only taking on and succeeding with challenges but also becoming knowledgeable in a supervisory capacity and learning how to interview and hire a competent person. I would both hire and fire many individuals during my career, and with each encounter, I would become more secure in my ability to supervise and manage. This competence may not have ever developed if I had not applied for a position that was probably above my experiences but was something I desired and felt would increase my chances of being successful.

I continued as the counseling supervisor with this organization for over a year and was successful in generating positive results within the department. I became increasingly popular with many of the management team that ran the organization and developed some social interactions with them. I suggested to my director, as a way to improve the morale of the clients, to open a small thrift store within the rehabilitation and sheltered workshop area. The synopsis of the idea was to award positive accomplishments of the handicapped clients, no matter how small the achievement, with paper money given to them by their counselors to be used to purchase items in this newly created thrift shop.

The idea was not original. I had used something similar, but with a different approach, during my teaching days to reward my students for extra effort. At times, using successful past approaches in new settings will produce quality results.

My idea was initially rejected by my immediate supervisor as too complicated. She felt the executive director would not accept the concept. I eventually convinced her to allow me to present the project to the executive director to seek his opinion on the idea. My supervisor, who was the director of rehabilitation, never wanted to "rock the boat" and would squash my attempts to improve the working environment by not allowing some of my ideas that I thought would be successful to come to fruition. I later found out that she had lost her enthusiasm for her position and was exploring joining a governmental organization in a similar capacity.

There are times when your ideas of improvement will come across with much less enthusiasm to your supervisor/manager. Don't let that curtail your efforts. If you are fairly certain that what you believe in will produce positive results, then go the extra step and approach a higher authority, hopefully with permission, and give it your best shot. Don't let negative influences prevent you from accomplishing your objectives that will benefit the society that you are engaged in.

Too many times, less than passionate managers hamper the ability of the employees to achieve success simply because it may be too inconvenient to "rock the boat"!

After agreeing to have me present my concept to the top guy, I approached him with some trepidation but also with confidence that my idea would be successful. I know it sounds like this idea of mine might not be earth shattering, but within this type of organization, changes or differences in the norm were rare. The organization has been around for ages and was steeped in tradition. New concepts were rarely attempted, even as minor as this little thrift store idea.

When I finally related my idea to the executive director, he asked several pertinent questions about the process and the execution of the project. After assuring him that I had covered all the bases before presenting the idea to him, he agreed to a trial period before becoming fully on board with the proposal.

With the help of several of the sales team personnel who thought the idea was a good one, I found a space in the building that would encompass a small, but viable, thrift store.

After several weeks of preparation and coordination, an attractive, but limited, thrift store was opened to our clients. It was received with enormous gratitude and appreciation from the handicapped workers that immediately used their paper money for purchases. The counseling department received a multitude of compliments and acknowledgements by the entire staff and especially from the sheltered workers who seemed to perform their menial tasks with renewed fervor so they would be rewarded with paper dollars.

The project was warmly endorsed by the executive director and eventually led to another promotion but in a much different direction. Without my intention, I was recognized for not only conceiving a new idea for the counseling area but also for my ability and flair for setting up and merchandising the donated materials within this limited space. I was commended for my efforts in the agency newsletter, and within a short period, promoted to a much more crucial position within the agency with a much higher salary. This promotion brought on much recognition but also much anxiety.

Sales Director

As I mentioned previously, within this large non-profit corporation were five medium-to-large thrift stores that produced all the income for the staff, sheltered employees, and all of the programs that assisted the physical and mentally disabled.

During my in-house thrift store process at the corporate building, the sales director who had been with the agency for many years decided to leave the organization to pursue a career in pharmaceutical sales. Therefore, the position of sales director became available. Again, without much expertise in this particular area, I decided to apply for the position.

Non-profit organizations tend to promote within, and my advance to higher-level positions may not have equated to the same opportunities in the business, corporate setting. However, if you are secure with your skills and abilities and feel that you are capable of taking on larger responsibilities, then go for the opportunity when it presents itself, even though your job expertise may not fit the description of the position.

I, once again, rearranged my now growing resumé and highlighted any sales experience that I had acquired. In addition, I was in the right place at the right time with my client thrift store project and the success it had generated. With this package of accomplishments, I was granted an interview with the executive director of the agency for the sales director position.

The interview went well, and I felt I had answered several of the concerns the interviewer presented. However, this position was held in high regard within the agency, and more candidates were brought in for interviews. Eventually, another candidate with a track record in sales was hired for the position. I was letdown initially but felt satisfied that I had given it my best shot even though I did not get the position. However, after a couple of months of mostly unsuccessful attempts for this new director to assimilate into the non-profit settings (he came from high end corporate sales) and his inability to relate to the store manager staff, a mutual decision was made. He resigned or was let go from his position (not sure which was the end result).

Shortly after his departure, I was called into the executive director's office and presented with the opportunity to take on the position with a probation period of ninety days. The caveat was that if I did not perform up to expectations that I would be removed from the position and be given the opportunity to remain with the agency in some capacity but with no guarantees that a desirable position would be available. He stated that these factors were the same stipulations that were presented to the previous candidate without the "remaining with the agency" part. I accepted these terms and was now the new sales director for the agency after approval by the board of directors and as long as I performed appropriately. (Was I thinking correctly with this acceptance?)

The ninety-day probation period came and went without any obstacles. I grasped the duties and responsibilities of the position fairly easily since I was now going into my third year with the agency. I knew the inner workings of the organization and had several social interactions with the sales staff that knew me as a fair and likable individual. However, I still had to win them over by displaying my abilities and producing positive results.

Many times the measurement of a manager's success is how they relate to the staff during the good and bad situations that will occur during the interactions with them. Initially, my concentrations were on the "nuts and bolts" of the non-profit sales business aspects. However, once I felt I had digested the intricacies of thrift store sales and how to increase the profits, which was no easy task, I then began to establish a positive rapport with the store managers to ensure that we were all on the same page. My past experiences with dealing with students, parents, and people in general in my previous employment gave me the expertise in handling different personalities. Once I had created a positive connection with the all-female management staff, I was able to become both a sounding board for their concerns and the person that would get results when needed. The working environment now became much more conducive to positive results.

The thrift store responsibilities were not the only aspect of this important position within the organization. My duties also consisted of coordinating with the transportation department the pick-up of donated goods from the public and the delivery of the appropriate items to the thrift stores. In addition, the agency employed the handicapped to sort, price, and pack clothing and miscellaneous items to be sent to the thrift stores. My coordination efforts dramatically increased with this position, and I needed to use my confident personality traits to cajole, beg, and sometimes demand that important tasks were accomplished adequately and timely.

The interaction with all levels of hierarchy within the agency and the multitude of personalities that I came in contact with was at a much higher rate then I had ever witnessed in any other position. I became more assured of my capabilities and expanded my competence by simply "learning on the job." I quickly adapted to the numerous different and unique situations that would come about almost on a daily basis. I was becoming an effective and efficient manager while remaining true to my beliefs of a guiding approach but with strong command when needed, instead of the authoritative path with no room for different approaches that I have observed from several managers/supervisors in

my career. I remembered where I came from and used my ability to connect with others to exhibit my reason for promotion while not letting
my success change my personality and demeanor. However, even with
this newfound growth of management skills, I still was unprepared to
conquer several other issues that would show their distasteful and unscrupulous nature when dealing with individuals who had little regard
for anyone but themselves.

While enjoying the success of being elevated in job statue and
personal growth, I was also indoctrinated into different cultures and
a working environment that required interaction with all types of personalities who had many different backgrounds. At this time, I became
infatuated with minorities, especially people of color. For the most part,
I was delighted with my broadened scope of rapport with all individuals I came into contact with that were part of the agency. However, I
don't want this to sound anything but complimentary and do not want
to offend any politically correct individuals that feel whenever you approach the similarities or differences in nationalities or races that there
is a fine line to establish. I just want to be truthful with my experiences.
I feel our country has become too politically correct at times and that
we should savor each other's positives and negatives if presented with
levity and respect and use humor as the equalizer to "getting along."
While working along and in conjunction with minorities, I developed
a real sense of the positives in all people and found myself enjoying and
expanding relationships, especially with African Americans. We would
laugh, learn, and grow in respect of each other in ways that you can't du-
plicate unless the working environment allows for this interaction. I experienced dating a lovely black girl during this time that was employed
at the agency and expanded my knowledge of both the similarities and

differences of the races. I remember this episode of my life fondly but also remember the stares that we would witness whenever we were out in the public view.

I often think of the many people that I came in contact with during the jobs of my life and the pleasant memories that I enjoyed with many of them. I would love to reconnect with some and let them know that I do remember the good times with them and hope they are doing well. Unfortunately, life goes on, and the positive interactions with others ends many times without ever knowing how their lives continued without your connection with them. Always keep an open mind while working with your fellow employees, no matter what their heritage or background might be, and don't let preexisting theories about others distort your relationship with them. Give everyone a "clean slate" and interact with them equally.

Although I was relishing in a self-confident and affirmative direction with my position as sales director, some unfortunate and downright offensive circumstances were presented directly toward my attention.

As I previously mentioned, I had established both workable and personal relations with several of my coworkers who were at my level and/or below my position statue. We would not only enjoy working together but would also go out after hours and party. One of these individuals, who I had previously hired as a job coach for the disabled clients while I was the counseling supervisor, decided he wanted my job. I thought we had a very friendly connection and had enjoyed several beverages together while laughing with others in a group setting that we all enjoyed. However, he somehow developed an adverse nature toward me and plotted against me by "bad mouthing" any of my endeavors to whoever would listen. Luckily, I had secured relationships with several of the individuals he supposedly confided, in and they let me know what he was erroneously reporting to others. In addition, a clear sign of his unscrupulous actions were obvious with his lack of eye contact whenever he was in my company.

Eye contact is something everyone should be aware of when working with others in any capacity. If an individual cannot, or will not, make sincere eye contact with you during even the simplest of conversations, then a trust factor might be part of the equation. Young people sometimes have difficulty in making eye contact with adults simply because they may be experiencing low self-esteem. As teachers/counselors/parents, we should encourage this in our youth so they will be prepared as adults to recognize that eye contact is important for establishing trust.

Although his negative words about me did not affect my ability to continue with my duties, it did induce some doubt in the minds of some individuals. I knew I had to somehow put an end to this contemptible approach by this envious and reprehensible character.

I contemplated with prayer ways to extinguish this awful attack on my personal well-being by attempting to continue to prove my abilities. However, I knew it was evitable that I would have to confront the culprit head on. Maybe it was luck or some type of higher intervention, or just the corrupt mindset of this individual, but very close to the day I was going to address the issue directly, the rascal was caught stealing merchandise from the organization. I remember clearly to this day standing alongside the executive director watching from a window on the top floor as this idiot loaded up the trunk of his car in broad daylight with merchandise that he and another cohort thought they would be able to sneak out. The director immediately fired him on the spot. We all then realized his intensions were not only to somehow get my job but also have access to his choice of any of the merchandise that would be allocated to the thrift stores for his use or resale. Many items would be sent directly to the sales director's office for distribution.

Recognize your strengths and be aware of your weaknesses within your working environment. Be confident of your abilities, but be aware of your possible adversaries. In this situation, I did not need to handle a distasteful circumstance but knew that if I had to encounter a difficult occurrence that I would with a strong will determined to right a wrong. Several of my positions during my life required standing up and having the determination to not let negative influences interrupt or deviate from my true positive intensions. I would present my views to co-workers and supervisors/managers/administrators with the upmost conviction when I knew I was correct in my assertions.

After this unfortunate incident, I continued to be successful in my position for about another year or so. During that time, the executive director that was with the agency for a long period of time decided to retire. He was viewed by most of the employees under his leadership as a difficult and overly demanding superior with a standoffish approach. Most employees were happy to hear he was leaving. I was one of the few that appreciated his allowing his subordinates to perform their jobs without much interference. However, he was a bit over the top with some who were not performing up to his standards.

The ending of his tenure coincided with the hiring of another individual to take over the entire responsibilities of the organization. This new executive director came in with a much different, friendlier approach that seemed to be a positive change for the agency. He presented himself as one who wanted to listen to others and develop plans to improve the surroundings, which was a refreshing change to the dictatorship approach that preceded him by the previous director.

However, within a short period of time, his willingness to listen and his supposedly thoughtful approach to change began to develop into a "know it all" mantra that became a disruptive and disturbing situation throughout the agency. If you were on his side and accepted his demands, then he would allow you to continue to do your job. However, if you were opposed to his ideas, some of which were outlandish, you were ostracized and berated as an incompetent or an unworthy employee. I developed a rapport with him knowing that he was now my immediate supervisor, and I would have to adjust to his leadership style if I was to remain in my position. However, I started to witness too many good people being ridiculed for not adhering to his every whim and began to realize that my position with the agency was at a crossroads.

Several board members of the organization were also aware of his negativity toward long standing employees as word of his poor management style began spreading throughout the agency. I remember a particular well-respected employee mentioning to me as many others were rejoicing with the retiring of the previous director that you never know what you have until someone worse replaces them.

These words ran very true in this instance. Within approximately six months, this new executive director had turned the agency upside down, and the individuals on the board of directors who had hired him began to make plans to "change the course" and looked to me as part of their strategy. This development led to yet another promotion but not without consequences that eventually ended with my leaving the organization.

Assistant Executive Director

I received a phone call one night at home from one of the members of the board of directors of the agency. He stated that he and several of the board members, including the president of the board, wanted me to join them for a short dinner meeting the next night. He mentioned that they would explain to me the details of this meeting at dinner but that I needed to keep this secret from all others in the agency, especially the existing executive director. My first reaction was one of disbelief. I had previously developed a rapport with this board member but not enough to figure out his intentions for this hush-hush meeting. I knew the board members were dissatisfied with the job the executive director was doing, and I had heard through the rumor mills that they were contemplating changes but had no idea that their plan included me.

The next day, I remember treading very lightly with any conversations about the executive director from others, which had become the norm since he had placed his imprint on the agency. I also almost intentionally tried to avoid any lengthy conversations with the executive director in case he had gotten wind of this new undisclosed development. I used the day to visit several of the thrift stores, which was a common function with my position.

At the end of the day, I began to foster trepidation about the outcome of this private dinner meeting. We met at the designated restaurant, and I was immediately notified that my dinner was going to be paid for by the board members. At this juncture, I was feeling very uneasy. (What was their intention, and how did it involve me?)

Once we all sat down the president and vice president who called me about the meeting began to praise my accomplishments within the agency during my four years there and recognized my loyalty with several of my positive achievements. I was very surprised that they were even aware of my past successes with the agency. I began to get a sense of excitement while listening to the compliments directed to me. In addition, they also began to downgrade the job that the existing executive director was performing and how they knew changes had to occur. They were promoting me to assistant executive director with the opportunity to attend the corporate executive director training. I was also to report directly to the board members while functioning under the supervision of the existing executive director.

Their rationale for my promotion was to assist the executive director in adapting to the non-profit system of procedures that were the backbone of the agency and be in place in case there was a need to make additional changes. Also, after executive training, I would be eligible to lead any of the other agencies in the country. I would use my experience in other positions with the agency by displaying the appropriate employee connections that I had developed to assist the executive director. In addition, I would indoctrinate the director with the training I would receive from the corporate offices.

My initial reaction was of gratitude and appreciation. However, anxiety began to develop due to the covert way this was being handled and the uncertainty of how this would be accepted by the current director. I asked several questions about what my new duties would be.

How was I to manage the reactions of the executive director who had exhibited egotistical approaches to many other situations? They assured me that they would be available for any concerns and that they would handle any uncomfortable situations that might occur with this new pecking order plan. The board VP stated that he would call the executive director after we were finished and present him with the plan they had developed.

With the ending of the meeting around 8:00 pm, I returned to my home with many thoughts of both concern and excitement. I was being elevated to a position of the highest rank, other then executive director, and would oversee the entire operation that included the rehabilitation, sales, personnel, and public relations departments along with assisting the director in his approach to employees and their needs. In addition, I would be trained at the corporate headquarters to become an executive director either at the existing agency or somewhere else. I was confident in my abilities to take on the added responsibilities of this promotion, but I could not stop thinking of how the director would react to this new development.

The next day, I would clearly and undoubtedly witness the reaction and backlash of the executive director in the most cruel and atrocious fashion. As I mentioned previously, many episodes in the jobs of my life began in a positive manner only to change into negative outcomes. This is another in a series of events that shook my being and made me question whether I was ever going to be a true success or attain my self-actualization goal.

The day after our back door meeting, the executive director greeted me with the most scornful facial expression and suggested we go out for a drive. While in his car and at his disposal, he proceeded to instruct me on the politics of life and informed me that there was no way the board was going to promote an Italian city boy to the position of executive director and that one way or another, he would not allow it. I attempted to come up with the scenario of working together to improve the agency and the rewards that would come with a successful plan, but he wanted no part of it. As far as he was concerned, I would have this new stupid title but would continue in the same capacity as previously, whether the board members wanted it this way or not.

I began realizing that this arrangement was not going to go smoothly to say the least. Every day for the next few weeks, he would berate my performance in every aspect that he could and simply made my life miserable. Most of my colleagues sympathized with me but realized they had no power to go against this egotistical maniac. Eventually, we had a closed door screaming session in my office, and at that point I told him I could not continue working in this environment, and I would begin a job search. He actually agreed to give me some time to find another position. Several high-ranking employees went to the board members and relayed what was happening to me, but no actions were taken. I also called the board VP to attempt some interaction on their part to help me with this dilemma, but even though he stated they would "look into it" nothing was done or suggested. I was on an island of my own and had to either sink or swim.

I guess the board's assertion was that with my resigning, I had given in to this shameless character, and maybe I was not a fit for their executive director training. I will never know the real reason that I was left to defend for myself, but I will always remember the anguish and utter devastation I encountered during my last days with the agency. I began thinking that maybe this was all a political move by the board, and maybe, as the director so distinctly pointed out, that it was never the intention of the board members to promote me but rather to witness the reaction of the executive director to the possibility of having someone helping him with issues his ego felt were under control.

Finding another position was not a difficult assignment for me since my resume' was now growing with promotions and successful accomplishments. However, leaving an environment that was very conducive to positive interactions and having attained various successful advancements, I was saddened to leave an organization that had treated me well until the end. I was also dismayed that I no longer would be working with the many associates I had met and became friends with even though we all promised that we would keep in touch.

A year or so after I left the agency and was employed by another non-profit organization, one of my close colleagues who was still at the agency informed me that the board had finally fired the executive director and that most of the remaining employees were thrilled with this result. However, to my dismay, the board decided to promote the rehabilitation director to the executive director position, which was viewed as a positive development by many of the employees. My friend stated to me that I should have been chosen to head the agency, but in reality, too much time had expired, and I was not even given an interview.

I have contemplated at times why my work life has had so many ups and downs, especially many that were out of my control. I think back about this episode and wonder how egos get in the way of possible productive outcomes. This character who was my undoing was one of the most conceited, pompous, and egotistical individuals I have ever had the unfortunate occasion to work with. How does a person become that dreadful without realizing they are the cause of their own downfall?

It boggles my mind when I meet people that have no idea of their inadequacies and deficiencies and really believe that there is nothing wrong or inwardly "out of place" with their being. (Look in the mirror, dammit!!) My advice to all that are attempting self-actualization is to look inwardly and outwardly to develop a true and honest approach to life. I know the world can't be made up of all purposeful individuals but life as we know it would be much better if people would only take the time to understand themselves and others and appreciate the time they have on earth. Anyone can change if only they would attempt to improve their life and be willing to not let ego and greed enter their souls.

During my journeys, I have made some good, and not so great, decisions about employment that affected my life in different ways. Sometimes the most promising development may end up being one of the most negative experiences, but living the experience prepares us to be ready for whatever is in store for us in our life's plan. Again, be the best that you can be, and see where your ride will take you!!

Director of Emergency Services and Military Liaison

Impressive title, right? Well, not really. Remember, I accepted this job with another well-respected non-profit organization in order to maintain my sanity. I did not have the time to make logical decisions about the next step in my employment. I simply had to leave the above position to escape the mental torture. I felt this position seemed to be the best opportunity in the short period of time that was given to me. I needed to recapture my self-worth. It was also located in the same area as my previous position (Camden, NJ), and the transition would be easier rather than having to interview in other areas that I would need time off to attend. I felt my departure from my previous position was somewhat due to my lack of maturity and awareness by not realizing what the board of directors real intentions were when they promoted me. I had to reclaim my self-esteem and realize that factors beyond my control caused my need to change positions and that I was still the self-confident individual that I knew I was.

Sometimes life will bring on some circumstances that make you "scratch your head" and wonder why and how did this happen to me. As I stated previously, you cannot dwell in the negative, although at times it may be difficult to gather up the strength and resolve to continue toward a success you feel is there but elusive. I experienced these feelings during this episode in my work life. As I suggested previously, it is always acceptable to find a job while still working at another. If time permits, and your resumé supports appropriate accomplishments, then take your time and research your options. Having to leave abruptly was my dilemma in this situation.

This new position was a one-man department (myself) that included working with a volunteer group that, at times, would drive me crazy! I initially attempted to be enthusiastic about the duties of the position but quickly fell into a routine of day-to-day activities that were not challenging or demanding.

The emergency services part of the position involved assisting the unfortunate individuals that would come into the agency seeking help with food and/or expenses. Unfortunately, the organization did not give immediate help to these poor souls but would refer them to agencies in the area that would address their needs. This was one of my duties but would afford me only the task of referring instead of direct assistance, which would have been my preference.

In addition, the organization was very involved with fires and disasters that would occur both locally and nationally. It was my responsibility to make sure we had the appropriate number of volunteers to assist individuals and families with necessities to keep them in surviving mode until they could reestablish themselves after a devastating fire to their surroundings. I do not in any way want to downgrade the importance of this real need in the community and the essential efforts that the volunteers performed. However, the volunteers were a rare breed, and their leader was an exceptionally unrealistic older man who expected everyone, including myself, to adhere to his every whim when it involved "chasing fires." He would drop everything in his "retired" life to go to the scene of need and expected everyone else to do the same. I understand these types of individuals are absolutely needed in times of need for the unfortunate ones involved in fires. However, his intentions and demands were sometimes "over the top" to a point that he tried to "bully" some of the other volunteers with guilt to attempt to elicit their time.

Therefore, after several realizations of not being able to adhere to his requirements, I finally established a working relationship with him and the other volunteers that would increase their effectiveness and allow my development as the director to focus on the overall responsibilities of the position.

I want to emphasize here that I was able to accomplish this reorganization of the volunteer staff and their responsibilities due to my past experiences in managing people. However, this accomplishment was not out of pride in my abilities but more due to my dislike of the working environment that I found myself in. I was not happy with my decision to accept this position but had no one but myself to blame. I felt this time in my working life was not going in a positive direction. I realized that I could have, and should have, handled things a bit more sympathetically with the volunteers. Unfortunately, with my displeasure of being in a position that did not afford me the challenges I was hoping for, I went for the easier approach, rather than the more complicated one of trying to figure out a more workable arrangement. I probably made things a little less palatable for the volunteers in order to simply get past what I felt was an annoyance. Yes, I was feeling sorry for myself with what had happened tome.

When I look back at this episode of my work life, I must admit to some feelings of regret for the way I handled my predicament. It is never wise to accept a position that you feel is not up to your standards unless you are desperate. However, if you do acquire such a position try your best to perform the "right way" and not to take the easy way out. This was not the approach I feel I chose with this encounter.

In addition, I was in charge of the communication with active military personnel and their families and loved ones. This was a very pleasant activity, and I enjoyed this part of my position. I felt that I was helping in a small way with connecting the families to the military when the need was identified. However, this was not a frequent occurrence;

this only occurred a few times a month when all other avenues of communication were extinguished.

In my previous position, I was in charge of large departments with hundreds of individuals under my supervision. I now found myself in a one-man department, in a small office with about ten people in various job responsibilities. It was a major adjustment for my psyche and make-up. I was used to making decisions on a much larger level and communicating to individuals in many different job capacities with various personalities. I enjoyed this active interaction and was successful in many ways. With this position, my supervision was very limited, and my communication with others had no relation to my job responsibilities, just simply "small talk" that exists in small offices. One reason I accepted this position was because of the possibility of promotional opportunities that this well-known, large non-profit offered. However, my hopes for advancement never came during my four years of employment there.

In addition, as is sometimes found in small office settings, this office was dominated by two women (nags) that viewed themselves as "owning the place." They would go out of their way, especially to new employees, to exhibit their own type of control by making it obvious that they were really the backbone of the office and the executive director was more of the figurehead. One was the director's secretary, and the other was the office manager. Certainly neither position was worthy of the importance that they felt (in their minds) they brought to the agency. They enjoyed making the employees around them uncomfortable by pointing out to everyone within earshot how someone had come in a minute or so late or left the office a few minutes early. They would also gossip regularly about employees in the office and some that would occasionally visit the office. The gossip would mostly be about something negative or unflattering and always, of course, when the employees could not defend themselves. Although this was difficult initially, after a period of time, I simply ignored them and tried to have as little contact with them as possible.

There will be times, especially in small offices, that certain individuals will attempt to upgrade their status by attempting to intimidate those they feel will be affected by the intimidation, to simply satisfy their egos. Do your best to "get along," but do not get caught up in this negativity. In this case, I chose the "ignoring approach," but if there is a better way of handling this type of office politics by reporting the inappropriate behavior to a higher authority, then that may be the best way to discourage this conduct. With this situation, the executive director was either oblivious or chose to ignore the unfortunate antics as long as the two female employees did what he asked of them.

Not everything about my position with this organization was detrimental to my well-being. After letting go of some of my negative energy from the unfortunate happenings with my previous employment encounter, I was fortunate to meet some extraordinary people during my four years with the agency. The organization is considered one of the best within its niche, and many of the people employed were dedicated to services they performed and presented themselves with the pride of belonging to an upstanding non-profit entity. Many of the individuals that I met will be fondly remembered but were outside of our intimate office. However, there were a few that I connected with within the office that will remain in my memory as exceptional human beings that I had the fortunate circumstance to work with and become friends with, but regrettably, have not continued a relationship with them. Hopefully, they are all doing well.

A real positive with this organization was the make-up of their board of directors. Several non-profits that I worked for before and since did not have board members that were interested in truly assisting or improving the agency that they represented. Too often, board members have their own agenda, either for political advancement or simply because they have volunteered their time and exhibited some type of business acumen or religious affiliation that allowed them to become board members. Many take on the responsibility to simply feed their egos. This organization's board members would be selected from their resumés that would accentuate their accomplishments and how they would be an asset to the non-profit entity requesting their appointment. From the onset, the board member would be assigned to a committee within their alignment of expertise to meet, discuss, suggest, and assist in implementing improvements to the organization. This served well to the selected members who now had the distinguished accomplishment of being elected to a prestigious board of directors and the organization benefitted with their competence in the area they were assigned. Many improvements, grants, and other positive actions were developed and achieved by the direct assistance of the board. Again, this was not the case with several of the board of directors that I served under and worked with in other positions.

After approximately three years with this organization, I found myself bored and defunct of challenges that I was accustomed to with several of my previous positions. I began contemplating a change of position once again. However, without any immediate direction toward changing my working career, I attempted to enhance the duties of my existing position by meeting with the executive director and explaining my desire to expand my responsibilities and to increase the challenges of the position. He was very appreciative of my honesty and began developing a project that might afford me an expanded role with the agency.

If you find yourself in a similar work arrangement and desire an upgrade or expansion of your responsibilities, it may be appropriate to speak with your supervisor and let them know of your desire to be challenged or upgraded. However, be certain that you are secure with your existing duties and that you honestly are eager to take on more. In many cases, this may increase your earnings but do not attempt this development simply to get more money. Be careful what you ask for, and make sure you can handle it. In this case, my salary was increased, but the assignment did not fit my intentions of being challenged and/ or upgraded.

The assignment was to be trained by an outside company and implement a new program for the agency that involved working with the older population with a medical assistance button. At that time, there were many TV commercials about an elderly individual falling and yelling, "I've fallen and can't get up!" The retail company that manufactured these medical alert buttons to be worn around the neck or wrist of the eligible client wanted to expand their territory of users by attaching the name of this well-known non-profit to their product. They were also willing to compensate the agency and the person in charge of the program within the organization. My part in this development was to be trained by the staff of the retail company in the use and effectiveness of this alert button and the benefits for the individual that would purchase the medical device. The executive director felt that I would be an appropriate candidate to focus on this new program and that this might expand and develop the duties of my overall position. I was appreciative of his confidence in my abilities and decided to take on the project in hopes that it would re-energize an enthusiasm for my position and possibly extend my time with the organization.

After several weeks of training with two very knowledgeable salespersons, I was ready to go on to the selling aspect, which was the real purpose of the training. As described in several other jobs in this book, I had not exhibited a successful sales acuity in other venues involving outside sales. Was I naïve to think this would work? However, with the backing of this company, and the distinguished name of the non-profit, I forged forward attempting to try the sales opportunity once again. In addition, the appointments were made with the company's sales force prior to the visit. The family or individual requesting the consultation sent in an affirmative reply to the company that they were willing to listen to a presentation of the product. I actually had some limited success with selling a few of the alert buttons, but the anxiety of the actual deed left me with distaste for the process. A family member who made most of the appointments, felt mom, dad, grandma, or grandpa needed this alert button to assure their elderly ones were properly assisted if a health emergency occurred.

If anyone has had to take care of their elder family member or relatives, you know the difficulty of attempting to assist them in something they deem is unwarranted. I recall when my parents were both alive and living together in their own home how resistant my dad was to anything that might ease his life. The generation gap seems to be much wider with the elderly who never had the opportunity to witness how technology has improved our lives. They often revert back to "the good old days" and not accepting what they never had. Several times during my appointments, I witnessed resistance by the elderly who needed the medical alert button but refused to accept their dilemma of needing help. However, there were a few who understood their situation and accepted their family's recommendation and were willing to accept the assistance.

Once again, I found myself unwilling to continue the sales position not because it was too difficult but more because it was just not my nature to force someone into something that they were resistant to whether they really needed it or not. I did not flat out end my sales duties, but again, began exploring changing careers while I was still employed. I centered in on my past experiences with retail in the thrift store environment and researched the possibility of owning and operating my own business. I was somewhat disillusioned by what had occurred during my non-profit experiences and examined the possibility of becoming my own boss. The theory was desirable, but the results were not at all what I was hoping for.

Chapter Six

On My Own

Owner/Manager

UPON EXPLORING DIFFERENT opportunities while still employed, the prospect of becoming my own boss became an attractive possibility for the next step in my employment life. I became captivated by the prospect of not having any supervisor, manager, or administrator above me to block my creativity or to adjust to someone else's ideas that may or may not be in tune with my beliefs. However, the anticipation of "on my own" was a scary proposition, and I needed complete support of my family to continue in this direction.

At this time, my wife was still working for the large computer company that was referred to earlier, and her salary and benefits were enough for our small family to live on. For anyone contemplating a similar approach of starting a self-own business, make sure you have an appropriate amount of income to sustain the period of time that it will take to establish a viable business, which can take several years, or the clear possibility that the business fails and an alternate plan needs to be developed.

Once my wife and I agreed to give this retail business possibility a chance, I dove head first into exploring, developing, and advancing toward this opportunity. After feeling confident that I examined all aspects of a small retail business both positive and negative, I decided to make the move of leaving the non-profit position that I was not happy with to an unknown, but exciting, new employment adventure.

Having been involved in sports all my life, I decided to use my expertise in the retail arena by pursuing opening a sports apparel shop which also included sports related equipment and screen-printing processing. Working for myself in a retail environment that I was very comfortable with was personally a dream come true. I thought this development in my life was the greatest thing since sliced bread!

I used my past experiences with the non-profit retail environment to locate an appropriate retail space and began the process of merchandising and displaying items I purchased from several wholesale companies that I easily identified through research tools. I eventually provided the retail customer with an inviting and interesting space that was viewed with positive results from the customers, management, and other vendors in the small-enclosed mall that I chose as my first venture into the world of self-ownership.

Prior to opening the business, I wrote a detailed business plan that served as a guide for how to proceed with my approach in the retail market. In addition, I attended several small business classes before attempting this bold move.

If you are thinking of possibly moving in the self-ownership direction, remember to do your homework prior to going forward, and realize that no matter how knowledgeable about this type of venture you have become, there is more than an even chance that a new business, especially in the retail area, will fail. Statistics have shown that many more small businesses fail than succeed. However, feeling my past experiences would assist me in this endeavor, I followed my instincts and went forward hoping this venture was my beginning into to the world of the positive rewards of self-ownership and possibly attain my goal of self-actualization.

In many situations, following your "instincts" may be the absolute appropriate course of action. In this case, my instincts were not leading me in the right direction, but the desire and commitment to succeed through my individual skills and abilities out weighed the probabilities of failure.

My first year in the business was a positive experience, which allowed thoughts of making it, despite the odds, enter my mindset. I remember my first Christmas season and how delighted I was when I sold basically everything in the store right before the closing hours for the holiday season. It was fun, it was rewarding, and although I wasn't setting the world on fire, I was pleasantly pleased about how quickly I had developed a customer base and how well my retail space was accepted by the customers and vendors throughout our small mall. Net profit was not a result during my first year, but I continued feeling that the business was going in the right direction. I was beginning to establish my place in the retail environment and my self-confidence was also on an upward swing, especially after my displeasure with my previous employment.

However, as my past history has shown, my positivity soon turned into negative developments. Unlucky or unwise decisions seemed to dominate my entire time in this self-reliant retail period of my life. One adverse incident after another left me devastated to the point of utter exhaustion. Every year of my retail experience, prospects that looked like they were improving the overall operations were shot down by un-scrupulous people; bad break events, and unfortunate decisions.

After my first year when things were looking bright, I decided to hire an outside salesman who approached me about sponsoring his soft-ball team. He seemed to have connections based on his "real" job, and his willingness to increase my business by spreading the name of the establishment for screen-printing orders and other sports equipment needs seemed genuine. For his time and effort, he would receive a per-centage of the profit on the sale, and I would help his softball team with sponsorship. It seemed like a perfect arrangement for both of us.

However, after some investigative research on my part, due to his lack of production but "over the top" bravado, I soon realized he was just a conniver attempting to accomplish his personal agenda. His true intention was only to outfit his softball team with excellent parapherna-lia and equipment in order to better his stature with his team.

After not getting paid for several orders that I put together for his team, I realized his corrupt intentions and fired him. The monetary loss was not so much to affect my continuation of the business, but the experience left me with an uneasy perception of what other traps I would fall into that might end up being disastrous.

If you find yourself in a similar dilemma, when trust is involved, be sure to be as aware as possible about what the outcomes might be. In this case, I trusted someone who was a complete liar concerned only about his agenda because I concentrated on the positives instead of viewing the entire picture in order to make a decision. I have wondered what makes this type of individual tick. How can anyone deceive and lie without any regard to others and knowing he would eventually be caught? I guess this is similar to the thieves that steal, time and time again, without acknowledging the inevitable result of being apprehended and the consequences of their actions. I just don't get it.

After overcoming this initial unfavorable incident, I attempted to enhance the retail returns by sinking more personal money into better and more attractive merchandise. This plan began to become a favorable approach for a while due to the customer traffic that was strong in this small, but viable, mall location. However, an alarming development was happening at a slow, but continuous, rate. Several of the larger and well-known retail establishments were moving out of the mall when their leases were over, and most of the smaller retailers did not understand why.

Management of the mall wanted to sell the entire complex to a developer who wanted to tear down the buildings in order to build more "exclusive" shops. However, management was not informing the majority of the vendors in fear that they would not honor their lease and attempt to leave all at once.

I began to question management's objectives, before knowing the actual reality, and attempted to find out the reasons of the business departures by polling the various vendors in the mall and the managers of the large retail stores to try to find out the intentions of the management. It seemed that no one knew the reasons for the departures, and the hope was that new and viable businesses would renter the unoccupied spaces in the mall. During this time, I became an active member of the vendor association, which was one of my several union affiliated experiences during my years of employment.

After a few weeks of getting nowhere in the pursuit of finding the truth, the small sized vendors banded together to fight to keep our small, attractive, mall opened and running. Due to my vociferous attempts to find the answers, my fellow vendors elected me to become the president of the association. (The prior president had resigned under the stress of what was happening to his small eatery at the mall.) I was beholden to the vendors for this appointment and accepted the designation of president with pride and hopefulness that I could make a difference. I began to relentlessly pester the manager on site with, not only the minor complaints from the vendors both in the small stores and from the managers of the larger stores, but also continued to attempt to conclude why some of these larger retailers were moving out instead of extending their leases.

The bottom line became clear without the management ever officially informing the vendors that this small mall was a thing of the past, and our time there was quickly ending. As the inevitable was approaching, I continued the mindset that I could make it in the retail sports area and began to look for another retail space that would help my business to grow.

I must take a short pause here in my employment story to relate an interesting learning experience that I obtained during my initial time with my retail business during my first few years of operation. I believe it was some time during the end of my second year of the business that I found myself a little "bored" with the day to day activities of the store and started to look for something else (a second job) to coincide time wise with the business and an opportunity to bring in additional income that I could reinvest into our retail establishment. I had hired a salesperson that I trusted to perform the daily duties during the slower hours, and I would concentrate on the busier times, which were enjoyable and not at all difficult.

Therefore, I sought to find a part-time spot that would utilize my background and some of the variety of skills that I possessed.

I found a position in the paper that was entitled Navy personnel instructor. The description of the position was for a person who had education experience and willing to work approximately ten hours a week at the Navy facility in Philly. The pay was an hourly wage that seemed to fit my needs, and the hours were flexible. I decided to send a resumé and apply for the position.

I received a letter requesting an interview about a week later. The interview process was something I had never before encountered. The female that interviewed me had a series of twenty questions and simply read one by one after each of my answers. All during this process, she wrote copious notes from my responses but very rarely engaged in any conversation other than articulating one question or statement after another. Some of the prepared statements/questions were very personal and covered an array of topics that had my head spinning in many different directions. The interview/interrogation lasted over an hour, and after it was over, I had the feelings of relief and accomplishment that I had endured this cross-examination and felt I answered the inquires with appropriate and knowledgeable responses. The interviewer stated that over 200 people had applied, and about ten applicants would be called back for second interviews for three positions that were available. However, I left the interview wondering why I went through that ordeal and questioned if I actually wanted to pursue the position if I was requested to come back. Within a week, I received a letter to come to the additional interview stage that would last a week long. Holy guacamole!!!

Luckily, due to my flexibility with the store, I was able to commit a week to this next stage of interviewing. My thought was that if I was selected as one of the three instructors that I might enjoy the teaching aspect of the position and still have the majority of my concentration on my retail business while increasing income to improve the business.

The first day, ten applicants appeared in a classroom at the Navy facility. For the most part, the day was an instructional training day about what was going to occur during the rest of the week. The instructor, who was the same person who had conducted the interviews, informed us that we were in for a difficult week and that we would be challenged with demanding scenarios during the interactive sessions for the next few days. We were warned that the sessions may be antagonizing and not for the faint of heart. By the end of the week, the selected candidates would be chosen and would need to give a short teaching lesson to several Navy personnel.

The following day, only eight candidates appeared (two had dropped out from the ominous instructions from the day before) along with an additional three individuals that were currently employed by the Navy as instructors. After a brief discussion about what was about to happen, the sessions began with the current instructors purposely confronting the candidates with imposing personal inquiries in order to solicit responses that would generate more divisive comments from them. (What did I get myself into?) This bombardment of purposely contentious debating continued the next few days. The rationale, according to the Navy, was to separate the "individual with inner strength" from the weaker candidates that could not withstand the daily negative input and supposedly would not be able to handle the difficult situations that might surface while performing the duties of the position. However, each day the employed combatants would slowly relinquish their hold on the sessions and allow the candidates to become more involved in the discussions and develop much better communication without the feeling of being attacked.

I became a very active participant in the discussions and began to take on this whole process as a personal challenge. However, toward the end of the week, I had made the decision to continue to the end but not to take on the position if selected simply because the military way of operating and the adherence to precision was not an environment that I wanted to place myself in.

I was proud to be one of the selected three to conduct a short presentation to Navy personnel, which would be an introduction to the duties that the position required. Using my extensive teaching experience, I successfully executed a training lesson to about twenty service men and women and encouraged interaction with the given topic. The session was probably the easiest assignment during the entire process.

When all was completed, I informed the leader of the operation that I was not going to follow through but thanked them for the experience.

I guess I was probably wrong to wait till the end to acknowledge my indifference with the process for these positions, but I did possess an accomplishment that I wouldn't have achieved if I had not completed the entire process. Was this an appropriate action on my part?

At times, challenges will come about even if the results do not equal the effort. After this experience, I felt a renewed vitality toward my self-assuredness and now believed I could accomplish anything I put my mind to and placed all my energies into my business to make it a success. The reality with the business was not a success, but the drive toward self-actualization became a dominant triumph that I knew I would achieve even though many obstacles prevented my eventual success. The stronger and more confident you can become, the better you will take on the struggles when they are presented, and the more capable you will be to overcome them. This was my mindset at this time of my life, and after experiencing this exhausting endeavor; I came away with a rewarding sense of accomplishment.

Now, back to the reality of the retail business. At this point, after realizing management's intentions of closing down our small mall even though they still had not officially informed any of the tenants, I still felt that I could succeed in my small business venture. I began to look for other locations that would hopefully allow the business to grow. I found a location close to my home that seemed a natural fit, which would allow me to spend the time needed to reestablish a customer base and focus on my family needs. The store space was much larger and afforded much more area for retail merchandizing, which equated to an attractive and well-stocked sports retail establishment. However, the move was several miles away from my previous spot, and I lost many of the customers I had developed from the small mall. In addition, the space, although now more inviting, was in a strip mall that was not clearly visible to street traffic, and therefore, the customer flow was much lighter than the enclosed mall.

Looking back at this selection of retail space, I probably chose a more convenient spot for my personal life as opposed to one that concentrated on customer traffic. If you ever find yourself in a similar situation, remember your true intentions with your business. Don't let outside influences determine your decisions. Examine your options and choose the environment that will best increase your business. This should be your main focus. My mistake was to choose a retail spot that I hoped would continue to improve my business, but a major part of my decision was the close proximity to my home and the benefits that the move would allow me. If you are fully invested in your business, especially in the retail market, find the spot that you confidently feel will increase customer traffic and sales. That should be your main objective.

However, I was determined to connect with the surrounding community and got involved in soliciting orders of screen-printing much more then in my previous space, which was more retail oriented. I began calling businesses and offering good pricing on all sorts of T-shirt and other screen-printing apparel merchandise. In addition, I sent out flyers to support my intentions of becoming *the* local business for these types of products. I would also attempt to make appointments to speak with perspective customers at their business locations to present my samples of work for their review and possible orders. I would use my natural positive personality to exhibit a sales approach that was relaxed and non-pressurized. Yes, I was again in the outside sales arena, which had not been successful during my previous attempts, but this time I was selling items I believed in and was for the sole purpose to increase my own business. Although the outside approach was beginning to reap rewards, it was hard work, and the retail end of the business was suffering.

During sometime early in the third year of myself-ownedventure, an attractive and very visible enclosed farmers market opened about five miles from my existing location. I decided to rent a small space within the market and now was the owner of two retail sports apparel shops and felt that I was indeed going to "make it" on my own. Of course, now with two spots came more responsibility, time, and expense on my part to manage and operate two locations. The decision to expand was initially a good one, and the customer traffic at the new enclosed market was fantastic. I began selling retail merchandise quickly at the market while continuing to attempt to establish the screen-printing aspect of the business through my other location. As the overall sales were increasing, my involvement with running both establishments increased twofold. I was constantly moving from one location to the other to make sure each spot was merchandised properly and continued soliciting for screen-printing orders.

With any type of self-owned business, make sure you have the time, energy, and determination to succeed. It is inevitable that the sole owner will work his or her butt off if they are truly committed to their business.

At this point, the two businesses were running at a "break even" status, which I viewed as a positive accomplishment. I seemed to always have cash in my pocket, even though the accounting aspect had not yet shown much profit. Let me also make it clear that I enjoyed this time of my work life immensely. I was working for myself (and my family) in a retail area that I had developed expertise in and felt a tremendous sense of self-worth that I was on an upswing in my endeavor. So why wasn't I successful in the end? Here comes the impending, but familiar, downfall that is my history in work life.

While enjoying limited success, I decided to expand my retail spot in the farmers market and doubled the size of the location. Again, the customer flow continued to be constant, and my sales retail gains were climbing. So far, I was making good decisions based on real situations and clear, well-thought-out ideas to help the overall business continue to grow. However, whether it was greed or just attempting to continue in a positive direction, I entered into a business arrangement that proved disastrous and ultimately became the downfall of the entire operation.

The retail end of the business was increasing, but the screen-printing end was becoming stagnant. I did not have the time to continue to develop this side of the business but had a definite desire to do so since the profitability for screen-printing was much higher than the retail sports apparel industry. In addition, around this time, my wife was given the proposal of a decent monetary buy-out from her computer company position, or she would need to relocate to another area far from home if she wanted to continue with the company. After much thought and contemplation, she decided to take the buy-out. We both knew she had the skills and abilities to easily find another position and the cash windfall would ease our financial concerns of the business.

With this influx of unforeseen capital, we both felt that this might be the opportunity to expand the business by investing a portion of the money to advance the screen-printing process. Up to this point, any screen-printing orders that I received were outsourced to wholesale companies that had the machines and space to print the materials. I would purchase the blank product from other wholesalers who would sell the commodity to retail establishments and then bring the appropriate amount of blank product for the order to the screen printer for processing. Of course, each aspect would be a charge to my business, and I was at the mercy of these wholesalers to produce the finished product on time and be attractive to the customer who placed the order. Something unforeseen happened here that seemed, at the time, to be the perfect match to expand and grow the screen-printing aspect of the business.

Very shortly after receiving the buy-out from my wife's ex-company, a woman who had a small retail T-shirt business at the same farmers market that I was in approached me about becoming partners with her and her daughter in their off-site screen-printing business since her son decided he did not want to continue their business arrangement. I was advised by several people who were aware of this possible partnership and others that simply were concerned for my well-being that this might be a mistake to go into business with a woman that I hardly knew.

However, I still felt that this was an excellent opportunity to help my business succeed, and I ignored the possible negatives. I felt no matter what the obstacles might be, I could make this work. The positives with the monetary investment and partnership on my part would come with a fifty percent ownership of the entire screen-printing operation, which included all of the machines needed to have an in-house processing wholesale business. This arrangement would save all the costs of out-sourcing the orders. The negatives that I put aside, feeling the opportunity was just too inviting, were going into a partnership with someone I didn't know and had heard some discouraging reviews about and the possibility of losing the investment money if this arrangement did not work out.

During this time, I was blinded by the positives and overlooked the negatives. I don't believe greed was the reason for my decision to enter this agreement, but rather my ambition to succeed, and the belief that the timing seemed perfect for the expansion. I was determined to become that self-reliant individual that would make my family proud and would move me closer to the self-actualized goal that I so desired.

Never allow your goals and objectives in your working life be so enticing that you cloud the reality in making important decisions. Too many individuals including the son of the woman recommended that I should not take on this partnership, but my passion to be successful led me to decide to go forward. Don't let this happen to you if you are in a similar dilemma.

Shortly after entering into this partnership, I realized I probably had made a mistake but still had the conviction that I could make it all work out. Since my initial space was not doing well in the retail sales, we decided to move all of the screen-printing equipment (which was extensive) into my original retail spot. Therefore, the retail aspect of this location ended, and the new concept was exclusively for screen-printing. We constructed a wall to separate a small area in front for walk-in traffic with a doorway to the larger part with all the equipment. My first hint of dissatisfaction with the arrangement was that the retail area that I had meticulously merchandized for customer viewing and purchase had now disappeared and was replaced by several printing machines, drying tables, waste containers, and other devices. This reconstruction would, hopefully, produce a multitude of beautiful screen-printed items for sale from customer orders but completely destroyed the retail possibilities.

Along with the excessive machinery came the artist who would produce the designs according to customer requests and would be paid separately on an hourly basis, through sale proceeds. Although the theory seemed to be a good one, the reality became a nightmare. The customer orders did not flow as projected, the artist that was key in producing the finishing product was unreliable, and the management and profitability of the entire operation fell in my hands completely.

The partner, who I was told had a strange personality and was advised not to go into business with, would not allow herself to see that we were in trouble from the start and refused to accept any responsibility. Therefore, due to my past experiences and strong reserve, I attempted to "right the ship" by working feverishly to keep us afloat. Again, I should have seen this coming prior to entering the partnership agreement, especially when I was advised by so many not to go forward. However, my determination to succeed in this case became a detriment to my rational thinking. If you find yourself in a similar situation, try to make more conservative decisions rather than looking at the "pie in the sky" as your guiding light.

Things became ugly quickly. I had a blowout argument with my female partner and soon realized that, sink or swim, I would have to figure this out on my own. However, with a small, but acceptable, agreement developed prior to the partnership, a clause was placed in our contract that would release either of us from any financial responsibility that was outside of the business, and that none of our personal assets would be touched if this arrangement did not work out or if the business failed. A lawyer drew up the agreement, and I would certainly advise any self-business venture be separated from personal finances when starting up. Know the difference between sole-propriety, partnership, and corporation status when documents are established prior to beginning a business.

As the overall business faltered, the bills and the calls from vendors wanting payment multiplied. I was at an all time high stress level, and again, all responsibility was on my shoulders since the other partner continued to refuse to shoulder any culpability. Every penny of my retail sales at the farmers market was used to pay for the expenses of the screen-printing side. I tried everything, including attempting to sell both aspects of the business, which included the two locations, all merchandise with retail fixtures and equipment, and the entire screen-printing operation. I placed an ad in the newspaper and thought I had a buyer but was informed by his people that the screen-printing equipment that I half-purchased and thought would make me a million was out dated and no longer used by the newer and more productive screen printers in the business. I could not get a break. I spiraled downward in confidence, personality, and overall self-worth.

After not coming up with any other alternatives, I decided to put another resumé together to find a position that would help me financially and allow me to deal with this crisis separately. I shortly found a viable position with another non-profit organization that would be my place of employment for the next ten years of my life, which will be detailed in the next chapter. However, I still had the tremendous weight of the business on my shoulders.

I must pause a little here to emphasize my displeasure with banks and lawyers, especially when you need them. When I was opening the business, I made what I thought was a relationship with a bank to take on a business loan which I paid off. However, when times were not so good, even prior to entering this nightmare of a partnership, the bank always had excuses or unrealistic demands to my requests for help and left me on my own to figure things out. At times, I was successful in mending the issues, but of course, with this dilemma, they wouldn't even have a conversation with me. Also, most lawyers couldn't care less about you as an individual unless you could provide them with some business. I was, unfortunately, referred to a lawyer from a friend when I started out thinking that our mutual connection would bring about positive results. There were times that I did need the lawyer's help, and every time I asked him for advice, he gave me ill conceived information because he was too far removed from my business and had many more important clients to feed him the money he and many lawyers so desire. Each time, as I was floundering and asking for his advice, he would simply tell me if things got really bad, I could always file for bankruptcy. He would then send me an outrageous bill for the few minutes I spent with him on the phone.

When selecting a bank or a lawyer in any type of business or personal venture, make sure you trust their judgment by sitting down and explaining your needs and making sure they understand what you want from them. Let them provide you with their fees up front, and don't wait till you need them to find this out like I did. Try to be as knowledgeable as possible about the ins and outs of your venture and hope you won't need attorney or bank assistance too often. The least you need them the better, unless you are very successful; then they will be all over you like a short coat to get your business and improve their profit. Yes, I am very cynical in this matter.

After trying every possible angle, I decided to take my irresponsible lawyer's advice and filed for bankruptcy to relieve the tremendous pressure of unrelenting financial stress. The type of bankruptcy I chose was the lesser of the two evils and would not touch any of my personal assets. It would require me to disburse any monies from the selling of merchandise/equipment to vendors through the court. A bankruptcy lawyer, who was, of course, making money from my misfortunes, was assigned to my case. I spent about three weeks selling most of the inventory and equipment at ridiculously low prices but was finally relieved that it was almost over. However, the total devastation and embarrassment was overwhelming. Although the bankruptcy lawyer informed me that this would all go away in five to seven years, I was still extremely upset that all my efforts of making it on my own had come to this unfortunate ending, and it was appalling to me. I had let down my family and friends who had helped me, and most importantly, myself. Bearing the guilt of this for five or so years seemed like an eternity to me. Having secured a position that allowed me to place my energies toward another endeavor certainly helped. However, it took years before I was able to accept this failure and go on with the rest of my working career.

This ends my episode of self-ownership. The good times were very worthwhile, but the bad times were ruthless. Even with the end results of this endeavor, I must say that if I had to do it all over again, I probably would have the same mindset. If I had never given self-ownership a chance, I would always have that desire to be self-reliant without any interference above me. Of course, I wish I wouldn't have made the mistakes or had so many unfortunate occurrences happen. However, no matter how low and depressed I was when times were at their worst, I lived through it and became stronger because of it. There are life lessons that sometimes shake your faith, but if you are secure, you can overcome adversity at any level. I was still convinced, despite what had happened, that I would gain that personal self-actualization I so desired.

Front Desk Clerk

Before I leave this chapter, I must relate another position that I acquired during my second year of self-ownership. As you may recall, I stated around that time I was getting a little bored with simply manning a cash register at the store. I attempted to find a part-time job that would help bring in additional income to the business and had applied but did not accept, the Navy personnel instructor position. Right after that situation, I applied and was hired as a front end clerk at a local YMCA. In addition, my intentions with this position were also to attempt to sell screen-printed T-shirts to members of this YMCA and make contacts with others.

The hours were in the early morning a few days a week, so I was able to easily attend to this position and then move on to my retail store at the mini mall. The position was a pleasure, and with my usual friendly disposition, I was a natural for assisting with the needs of the members as they entered the facility to exercise, swim, or participate in the numerous classes provided to them for their membership. I have nothing but fond memories of the fellow workers, management, and participants of the facility. I made a few screen-printing sales during my time there and felt appreciated for my time and work within the agency. However, after about six months, the early arrivals got to me, and I decided to leave simply because I have a difficult time with getting up early. This has remained with me throughout my working life and even though several of my positions required being in early and on time, I still to this day have difficulty with waking before 9:00 am. Thank goodness I'm now retired! Ha!

Chapter Seven

Non-Profit One More Time

Stores Director/General Manager

As I PREVIOUSLY mentioned, I had secured a position with another non-profit organization prior to the demise of my retail business. The organization was based on a religious foundation, and its purpose was to help those in need. I was brought into the interview with the president of the board of directors who was attempting to upgrade the non-profit business aspect of the agency.

The inner workings of the business side of the organization was similar to my previous non-profit entity but to a much lesser degree.

There was a processing center and a few thrift stores that sold donated materials to the public and in turn assisted the needy. The concept was a redeeming feature and served well in my attempt to increase my self-confidence after the retail sales disaster. The elected, volunteer board president was a truly committed religious gentleman but also an entrepreneur who owned his own business. He realized, in order to increase the income, which would eventually become assistance to the poor, he needed to enhance the retail operation and separate the religious aspect from the business part. The previous director for the position I was interviewing for, was much more religious oriented and moved to a position within the agency that concentrated on the assistance facet.

The interview consisted of a short explanation of the organization's purpose and the ideas of how the president wanted to expand the retail operation. After a brief tour of the processing facility, which was a three-story building in one of the lowest economic areas in Philly, we got into his car and visited the four small retail thrift stores that were currently in operation. My initial reaction was skepticism about how anyone could take over and make this operation profitable. However, the challenge to turn the operation to a successful one could be a very rewarding accomplishment for both the organization and my inner desire to increase my self-worth.

After the interview, I researched the national organization and came away with the feeling that this might be the next step in my employment history. If you have a desire or opportunity to work for a non-profit institution, make sure you research the relevance of the agency and what exactly makes them "non-profit. There are several places of employment that act as non-profit entities but are really for profit companies hiding behind the non-profit name.

Within a week of the interview, I accepted a decent financial offer from the president and secured a position that would encompass the next ten years of my life. Soon after this decision, I ended all aspects of my retail business except for the anxiety from the result.

The position's responsibilities encompassed all the business aspects of the organization with approximately fifty workers under my supervision. I was back in an environment of communication, rapport' building, and complicated decisions. I had complete authority to change, replace, and enhance the current procedures using my previous experiences in similar operations to produce positive results. I felt confident in my abilities and realized that, with the organization's current business status, there was plenty of room for improvement. The next ten years of employment would produce very positive results, but as usual, also some agonizing developments that would be part of the territory.

My first year or so was spent on attempting to convince the employees that I was here to stay, and my mission was to turn things around in a positive direction. I also had to prove my integrity, gain their confidence, and in addition, rid the organization of those who were part of the reason why the business side was currently going in a negative direction. I had no problem that there was a huge ethnic difference between management and the workers and was committed to gaining the trust and respect of the employees. I have always made it a point to treat everyone on an equal basis, no matter the background or ethnicity of the individual, but needed to convince the workers that I would adhere to this approach.

Without much dissension, I developed a rapport with the individuals at every level while focusing on separating the "good" people from the unfavorable intimidators. Some of these antagonists would be the leaders in certain areas in the production department and would force their will on those who were simply trying to make an honest living. Having donated materials from the public as the sole income generator led to excessive theft by the employees whose rationale would be that if the materials were not paid for by the organization, then theft was actually a given. Of course, this way of thinking had to be stopped, or greatly reduced, if the business aspect was to be successful. With the type of organizations that involve donated materials, curtailing theft completely is almost an impossibility, but attempting to diminish the mindset is a necessity. This philosophy was my constant approach throughout my years with this organization.

Once the goals were set with the production area, I focused on the tremendous amount of used, sorted clothing and other donated materials that were being stored on the third floor of the production building to be eventually distributed to the four small thrift stores. It was obvious that the stored materials far out distanced the need for the inventory for the stores. Therefore, with the help from some of the other managers within the national scope of this non-profit, and the willingness of wholesalers to buy the used clothing in bulk, I decided to pursue this path and developed connections in the bulk clothing world. Immediately, income came pouring in which allowed me to further establish my sincere intensions to elevate conditions at the warehouse and get the business side on level ground. The bulk clothing aspect served the organization quite well during most of my tenure and brought on many advances in overall operations. However, the retail facet of the operation also needed a restructuring from top to bottom.

My quest was to expand both the amount and size of the stores and also bolster the amount of materials donated to the organization from the public. Again, using my past experiences with non-profits, I was able to increase the donated materials base. I began closing some of the smaller and unprofitable stores and opening larger, merchandize appealing stores in areas of need but not far from more affluent neighborhoods to help with donations. Now, with increased dollars from the bulk clothing industry, I was able to hire individuals that would be able to assist the operation in contacting the good people that were willing to donate their used textiles. For their donations, the public would receive a legitimate tax write-off, which was appealing for the urban well-to-do population. In addition, through the organization's volunteer base, destitute individuals and families would be given assistance anonymously with the proceeds from the business side and direct assistance from the public. We were now growing as an organization within its local boundaries and began becoming a noticeable entity within the scope of the national grouping, which encompassed many cities throughout the country.

With the backing and encouragement of the president of the organization, I was able to open several stores and expand a few of the existing stores. The process with each proceeding was time consuming and arduous, but I was devoted to accomplishing our goals and worked extremely hard to make this entire venture a success. I guess my retail business failure had a direct influence on my total commitment for this organization, which I believed in and served as almost retribution to my collapse from my sole owner retail experience. I felt, if successful, the needy would be assisted, my self-worth would increase, and my internal goal of self-actualization might be attained.

As is always the case, over the years, there were several episodes of difficult situations revolving around the positives that were happening within the organization. From massive theft, to employees that were not loyal, to a overly zealous religious staff member who wanted my position, to board members who had no knowledge or expertise about what they were supposedly advising, and some other unfortunate encounters; were some of the stumbling blocks that were needed to be overcome. Some situations were much more severe and complicated than others and resulted in some very heavy bouts of anxiety, but in the end, each negative occurrence was either conquered, thwarted, or ignored for the benefit of the organization. More on this board member atrocity later in this installment.

With the influx of income and expansion of most operations within the business aspect of the organization came the need to move from the outdated facility to a larger one that would be able to accommodate our growth. Therefore, I concentrated, with the assistance of our ambitious president, on finding a facility that would afford continued growth and increase the stature of the organization within the community and with the non-profit national scope that was an important step toward improving all aspects of the organization. After a year or so of looking for the appropriate facility that would update our growing needs, I found a building in a neighborhood that bordered on the low economic area that the organization assisted and the upscale area that would produce much of our donation base. This site was a huge undertaking but a positive move toward growth, and hopefully, stability. Once all the papers were signed by the banks, the real estate people, and the president of the board, we were set to move the entire warehousing operation to the new facility and close up the previous building which no longer served a purpose with the organization. However, the move was not without some tedious, and unfortunate happenings.

Of course, a move of this nature normally would be time-consuming and exhausting. Due to the type of business and the need to turn things back to operational quickly so not to prolong the needs of the thrift stores, we moved within a few days. Unfortunately, some of the surrounding community that felt we were abandoning them with both assistance and thrift store accessibility decided to give us a send-off by firing several bullets into the office area. Thankfully, no one was there at the time. Therefore, there was a newfound immediate rush to vacate the building and hope the shooting culprits would not follow us to the new building. Several good employees were lost because of the fear of retribution from the thugs in the neighborhood.

The move eventually was completed and the warehousing operation surprisingly was back and running in a short period of time. The layout and positioning of the departments within the 35,000 square foot building was something that was designed and in place several weeks prior to the actual move. We had a dock area for larger trailers to move in and out, a bulk-clothing component, a processing area, and also an established area in the front of the building as a neighborhood thrift store. The store provided assistance to the needy and a retail space for the purchase of clothing and other materials with little monetary output for the community. The office space provided areas for the religious component to be housed and an extensive office area in the back section of the building to be used as offices for the business side of the operation. This area also included a more than adequate office for myself. With this expansion, we needed, and had, an office set up for a financial accountant type and several other additions to allow continued growth.

Of course, there were bumps in the road, and employee hires that were either just bad decisions or just not the right person for the job's responsibilities. There were more and more decisions needed to be made under my jurisdiction then at any other time in my working life. The growth of the organization was at a rapid pace, and with this advancement came more and more responsibilities on my part. I was enjoying my rise in stature but continued to realize that there were always negative possibilities that could occur with so many variables within the operation.

The first few years of the expansion proved the rationale of the move and upgraded the assistance to the needy that was the backbone of the organization. However, as always, the good times were not without the adverse occurrences. Unscrupulous employees, continuous theft, second-guessing board members, and other situations were constant interruptions to whatever successes the business side was attaining. At this time, however, I was also promoted (in title only) to general manager of the business side of the organization. I was proud of the promotion but was performing the same, or much more of the same, duties when my title was stores director and received no additional monetary compensation for the promotion. The title coincided with the national scope of individuals that were in the same capacity as I and responsible for similar functions in other cities. I was, at one point, the director of a warehouse manager, a stores director, a procurement specialist, a financial accountant, a personnel manager, numerous supervisors, and about a hundred front-line employees. In addition, five large thrift stores were also under my umbrella of supervision. This, by far, was the highest stature that I had ever attained in my working world. In the non-profit circles, I was in the "big time."

Personally, my self-worth was now rising rapidly, but I still was not at the position in my life that I could say I was completely self-actualized. There were too many possible downfalls that could occur, and even though I was in a nice position in my working life, I never felt at peace within.

However, I managed the operation with the same intense and devoted approach as I exhibited in some of my past positions. I treated each and every employee in the same way as I would want someone to treat me. I would make a point to visit each area of the warehouse on almost a daily basis and spoke to not only the supervisors but also the individual employees that worked on an hourly basis. At times, I would work side by side with the employees, especially in the warehouse thrift store, to become a person that they would feel comfortable to approach if a problem was occurring. In addition, I frequently visited our five thrift stores to make sure the managers of the stores and the staff all were aware that I was approachable and took time with each to listen to their input.

The organization's main focus was to help those in need, which included the poor and downtrodden. However, the local and national constituents who were volunteering their time too often did not look within their own operation and attempt to assist our workers who were mostly on minimum wage. As the operation's income grew, I would attempt to increase wages of the hourly employees and developed a share cost medical program to offer as an important part of their salary package. I felt a need to improve the conditions of the working environment with material upgrades but also attempted to boost morale and promote advancement within the organization by having monthly staff meetings to discuss the issues.

Managers/administrators should all manage and supervise with the mindset of "do unto others as you would have others do unto you." This was a staple phrase recited frequently by my mother as I was growing up in South Philly, and I would always refer to this phrase as my theme when managing others. Managers need to drop their egos, remember where they came from, and manage others the way they would want to be managed. The individuals that run the ship are entitled to respect and appreciation for their efforts. Supervise with guidance, patience, and with the willingness to realize that the manager does not have all the answers, and a mutual cooperation is the best way to success. Managers should be part of the engine that will be responsible for putting the pieces together but not forgetting the individuals' contributions that allow the engine to operate. There will always be periods of negative experiences with operations of the size I was managing (like firing incompetent employees and dealing with the public), but hopefully the rewards will out distance the adverse situations.

Board member interference was one of the constant conflicts to the business side of the operation. Many of the board members who were elected to their positions simply because of their religious affiliation and their volunteer spirit without any or little expertise in the non-profit sector would use their capacity of board membership to come up with opinions that, for the most part, either did not make sense or would be the absolute wrong avenue to explore. No matter how my extensive background or experience in non-profit business was presented, their opinions would need to be scrutinized until proven wrong, in most cases, because of their standing as a board member. It seemed that I was always on the "hot seat" whenever I would be at a monthly board meeting.

Why are board members positions NOT always occupied by individuals who are there to assist the entity they supposedly serve and have expertise in areas that will improve wherever the organization has the need? Too often, board members are in their positions because they volunteered or were elected to either support their egotistical personalities or because of their religious affiliation, political aspirations, or financial gain. Board members should be proud to be elected or selected and should be involved with the interactions of the organization with a solid background in whatever discipline that they could offer. Otherwise, step away and let the experienced personnel make the important decisions.

I would attend bi-yearly meetings with the national organization's business contemporaries and would learn and develop strategies that were proven approaches by other operations within the scope of the national organization. I would then utilize what I had learned and developed from the national level and implement many of the positive ideas when I returned to our local operation. I became a well-respected and knowledgeable participant on the national sales committee and was viewed as an important component to the success of the national organization by many other non-profit business staff throughout the country.

Many of my fondest memories were made during these gatherings of the national scope. Several of my national sales area contemporaries from many cities throughout the country would band together to discuss various approaches to our unique environments and share thoughts and ideas with each other. Of course, after the meetings, we would congregate in the hosting city's better drinking establishments and somewhat continue our discussions but with louder and funnier language and with tons of laughter from the stories and anecdotes that were exchanged as the night wore on. I was awarded tremendous respect from the other GMs for my ability to turn around a downward operation into a growing, advancing enterprise that was admired by many throughout the country.

Locally, this feeling of pride in accomplishment was only recognized by the few that were "hands on" with the operation but not from the majority of the local board members and other individuals that were part of the religious side of the organization. Most knew we were supposedly doing well but didn't take the time or effort to find out. Personally, I knew the efforts of the inner circle of the business side were true and real to the success of the overall organization. Certainly, an inner satisfaction within was strong and conclusive to my ego and self-worth, but I never felt that I was truly accepted for my abilities from the organization's local constituents and board members. Therefore, even though I was at a higher level of personal self-confidence, I still did not have the sense of self-actualization that had been a constant goal throughout my working and personal life. There was always times that, as the top guy, I would be put on the spot for anything and everything that would not go in a positive direction from the local members and from the massive amount of donors and customers who would complain constantly about everything imaginable. However, I used these occasions to develop a strong and confident approach to the complainers and was usually able to eliminate the problem or at least calm them down with quick and decisive actions. I've used this ability to appease and alleviate problems, especially with parents in my next employment position.

No matter how many years you work or how many jobs you have, learning new and different approaches can be used in other environments to produce positive results. Develop, learn, and expand your challenges into a "bag of tricks" to be utilized at appropriate times in other avenues when job change is on the agenda.

For the most part, several years went by with continued growth and success but not without several adverse complications with many aspects of the operation. I was responsible to make sure the amount of money for payroll would be available on a weekly or bi-weekly basis, paying the bills that were constant and continuous, and completing budgets that were, hopefully, real and achievable. The weight on my shoulders was heavy, and I had to possess total commitment in order to accomplish the objectives of the organization. Luckily, the bulk clothing market remained strong for several years, and several of the thrift stores were performing well. However, we were always waiting for the next "shoe to drop" before we could just reap the rewards of the positives.

I was still very much appreciative of our accomplishments and enjoyed my stature with the organization. In addition, I became close with several great people, both locally and nationally, that I have, unfortunately, lost contact with but wish them well throughout their remaining lives.

One of the negatives about moving from one position to another for whatever reason is that too often the really excellent individuals you come across in your career move on without continued contact and are only short episodes in your life.

There are many working colleagues that I will always refer to as true friends, even if the time with them was short-lived. I often wish that I would run into some of these wonderful people I have met during my working career just to again let them know how much I appreciated the good times we had and will remember their friendship for many years to come.

While at probably the top of our growth, an unfortunate incident developed that would be a defining moment to my working career and my management style.

A production manager was fired for unruly behavior by the board president several months after the move to the new facility. Although this person was intelligent and valuable to the organization, he had a nasty streak that would serve as his demise. About a year or so after this episode, I made a major mistake of hiring back a trailer driver that I had previously fired for some of the same reasons as the previous production manager. The driver stated that he had fallen on tough times and had contacted me to give him another chance with the organization. He relented that he had learned from his mistakes and needed his job back in order to straighten out his life.

Many of the workers in the organization were given second chances after short term incarceration, bouts with the law, or going through difficult times in their lives and needing help attaining employment. This second chance approach toward employment fit well with the philosophy of helping the needy, which was the organization's main focus. (You will not find this approach in most of the for-profit companies who will scrutinize their candidates and only hire the exceptional ones and never rehire someone who was previously fired.) Therefore, I hired this individual back out of this second chance approach, completely unaware of his true intentions for returning to the organization.

The previous production manager and this individual were close friends, and a union takeover was being orchestrated from outside of the organization by these unscrupulous characters as revenge for their firing. The rehired trailer driver and another disgruntled employee working in the warehouse area contacted the local union affiliate with the help of the fired production manager in order to attempt unionizing the non-profit entity.

During my long working career, I have been associated with unions in several capacities with some positive and some negative reactions towards them. However, the type of union presence that we were dealing with in this situation was not going to be productive in the non-profit setting, and in my opinion, were more interested in collecting dues rather than helping the employees.

Most non-profits of the type I was managing do not receive income on a regular basis, and must rely on the public for donations. Retail companies, who have defined profits that may not be distributed to the masses in the most appropriate way, may need union affiliation. With many non-profits, the financial line is so narrow that any deviation may set off disastrous results. This was the situation with the union attempt with our organization.

Unfair practices or detrimental proceedings that would affect the well-being of the employees, along with wage salary disputes, might be cause for the need of union merging into a company that mistreats its employees. This was definitely not the case in our non-profit environment. We were not the leaders in salaries and benefits but were relatively comparable to many of the profitable industries in the area, and again the non-profit world was much different then the retail or for-profit arena. However, what we did possess, as I mentioned earlier, was an open atmosphere of communication and fair treatment of employees. At least, that's what I thought I was promoting throughout our organization. A union vote from the employees to management would be a definite message of whether my understanding of the welfare of the employees was real or misunderstood.

Our organization was now under new leadership, and a novice board president took over for the previous president because his term had ended. This was the first time I was to answer to a different person, other than the president who had hired me and worked closely with me at every turn. The gentleman who was now our president was another religious and dedicated individual, but with little preparation for this undertaking, especially during this union attempt on our organization. I had some sympathetic colleagues that were part of our management team that supported my efforts, but basically, this was my problem to deal with.

However, the new president was smart enough to hire a good labor lawyer in order to direct us with what was to become a long and overwhelming period of time filled with anxiety and suspense that would be placed mostly on my shoulders.

I had no idea what to expect from this entire episode and had no experience on how to handle the adversity. I was astonished at the lengths these union rascals would go to in order to win the vote of the employees. The president and myself attempted to solve the alleged issues by meeting with a few of the union reps and their attorney. The union dudes made it very clear at this meeting, with their union embroidered jackets, that there was no solution other than at least a month's worth of organizing and coordinating an employee vote to bring in the union or not.

At that point, the labor lawyer was brought into the organization to prepare us for this onslaught of negative and disparaging barrage of inaccurate material mostly focused in my direction. The labor lawyer instructed me that, as the perceived head of the organization and the familiar face of leadership, that I would be deluged with negative publicity that would be either made up or simply lies in order to convince the employees that they needed the union. Initially, I did not want to believe that this character assassination was actually going to happen, but within a short period of time, we witnessed the most outrageous and disgusting attempt by these union thugs to persuade the employees that their affiliation was needed. Letters and flyers were distributed to the employees stating negative things that never happened, and at every turn presented me as the culprit and cause of the indiscretion. The mistruths and lies were abundant, and it was beginning to affect my psyche. I was completely stressed out but needed to continue to attempt to keep the ship above water and running properly.

For the most part, the employees performed their jobs appropriately, and there was little discussion of what was happening whenever I was in their company. It was the proverbial "elephant in the room" atmosphere. It was also my job to somewhat answer and explain the discrepancies and lies perpetrated by the union reps in the form of letters disseminated to the employees. Although I was confident in my management style, and felt the employees would see through the dishonest maze that the union was presenting, but I could not be sure until the actual vote was conducted. The vote would also, in management's viewpoint, decide the destiny of the organization. We truly felt that, if the union takeover were successful, the fate of the business side of the organization would be in great jeopardy and possibly end completely. I tried to perform my extensive duties as usual but as you can imagine, my thoughts were constantly on what the voting outcome would be and how the result would affect the entire business side of the organization.

After a long period of counter attacks from both sides, the time for the actual vote was upon us. I can easily visualize the setting even now. We were in the cafeteria area, management on one side sitting at a table, and the union bullies with their union jackets, (which I guess was their preferred daily attire) sitting at another table across from us. As each and every individual employee came in to the cafeteria to cast their vote, the uncertain atmosphere was excruciating while waiting for the anticipated results. A neutral judge was brought in for the purpose of announcing each vote. As the votes were counted, it was obvious from the start that the employees voted for management and against the union. In fact, before all the votes were tabulated, the union reps left the building. Management had won overwhelmingly, and a cheer was heard from several of the employees who had waited around to hear the final results.

Initially, I was tremendously relieved. We had avoided what management perceived as almost a "life or death proposition" and could breathe again. More importantly to my inner-self, I felt a reprieve from the constant stress of the unknown and a renewed certainty that my management style worked and that the employees appreciated my attempt to make the working environment a fair and at least adequate place to be employed. The overwhelming number of positive votes from the employees toward the organization was the icing on the cake.

A few weeks or so after the union vote, and after the conversations about it had died down, I made it a point to meet with every employee that voted whether for or against and pledged again to continue my efforts to make the warehouse a better place to work. I was once again back to my commitment to continue to work toward success for the betterment of the organization and be aware of the individuals that were the true assets of the operation. The results of the union defeat was also heard at the national level, and I received messages from several GMs around the country congratulating my efforts and wanting more information about how this all came about and how we were able to overcome the takeover. I was happy that this episode was behind me, but I knew there were always going to be more stumbling blocks presented and hurdles to overcome with the type of position that I occupied within the organization.

Several weeks after the above matter was over, the new president of the organization resigned due to health issues. He also admitted that he did not realize the tremendous effort needed to take on the challenges of the presidency. Therefore, the previous president again took on the title. I was pleased and supportive of reuniting with the individual that hired me and reestablishing the working relationship that existed between the two of us. However, even though I had a tremendous respect for him, and appreciated his outlook toward our goals, he was not an easy person to work under. He was demanding, persistent, and sometimes overly critical, but in our working relationship we always had a mutual respect for each other's expertise. We would often butt heads on decisions to be made and the ways to go about daily processing, but we were always able to come to an agreement when needed. He was the constant in my working environment and a mentor in my efforts to improve the organization.

During this restructuring of leadership, the bulk clothing market began dropping in worth, and therefore, affecting our income in a negative fashion. We now had to move to again reestablish and improve our thrift store operations. The bulk clothing downfall also had a trickle down affect to our warehousing operation and overall thought process toward the continuation of our success. Several good employees were let go due to budget restrictions but were assisted with unemployment compensation in order to soften the blow and allow them to find other employment. Having the responsibility of giving an employee a pink slip, whether for being fired due to an egregious event or for budget constraints, is never an easy task. Unfortunately, one of my position's duties was to be the person involved in this undertaking. I was decisive when needed, especially during firings, and sympathetic during the lay-offs with a real effort to help with the laid off employee's next step.

The results of the plunging bulk market was debilitating, but I was determined to continue my resolve of leading the organization in whatever avenue was best for the overall operation. However, after another year or so, our board president again ended his term realizing that it was time to step down and let others get involved. I absolutely understood his intensions and supported his decision but had the feeling that my time with the organization was also dwindling.

A new president was elected by the volunteer base and began his term with the organization. From the start, I felt a negative vibe from him. He came from the retail for-profit world, and his knowledge and grasp of the non-profit industry left much to be desired. His ideas and plans worked well with some, but my experience and expertise led me to realize his concepts were misinformed and ill conceived. I attempted to explain my reasoning but to no avail. There was little respect for the many years of non-profit management experience I had attained. I could see the writing on the wall and began to contemplate the thought process of leaving the organization. I had placed all my working energies and strong resolve into the organization for ten years, but as was my history, my time had come to leave and seek another position or career that somehow would lead me to my elusive self-actualization goal. This was not an easy decision, and I did not want to leave one position until I had secured another. I was now fifty years of age, and although I had demonstrated tons of skills and abilities during my working career, the age factor might be a detriment. I decided that it might be my time to return to the education environment, which at one time was thought to be my work destiny.

While still working with the non-profit organization, I applied to a few school districts to become a school counselor. My completion of my master's degree in counseling from years past served as the piece that allowed the school districts to call me for interviews. After attending several interviews for a school counselor position, I realized and was informed by some of the interviewers, that although I had tremendous real world experience, I didn't have any actual in-school experience as a counselor. It was a combination of no longer feeling secure and appreciated in my non-profit position and my desire to, if given the chance, change careers once again and return to education for, hopefully, the rest of my working career.

Therefore, with an unsure future, I resigned my position with the non-profit and entered another uncertain time in my working life.

Just a short follow-up; I somewhat continued to be in touch with some of the good people that I worked with at the non-profit for about a year or so after I had left the organization. During that time, the organization suffered tremendous set backs and losses in revenue. The individual that basically took over my position with the organization was fired for indiscretions that I was not fully informed about, but his actions were deplorable enough that his firing was proved to be legitimate and conclusive. Although, over the years, I have completely separated any connections I had with anyone associated with the existing organization, I heard through the grapevine that hard times had befallen the non-profit and the management, and leadership of the business side had fallen back to mostly a smaller and less viable operation. However, I have not heard any news whatsoever about the current situation of the organization and certainly hope that they are on solid ground with the business side. I do know for sure the organization was strong and determined enough to continue their fine works with helping the needy.

I did not take any pride or pleasure in hearing what had become of the non-profit organization that I gave so much of my time and effort toward. However, I use this unfortunate outcome to remind those placed in decision making positions as administrators, managers, principals, etc., to be mindful of the workers that have past experiences and knowledge, and utilize their expertise when decisions, compromises, or judgments are to be made. Don't reinvent the wheel if it doesn't need to be adjusted or changed. Listen to your staff. Take their assessments into account when changes are needed. Visit their workplace, their classrooms, their offices, not always as a supervisor telling them what they're doing wrong, but as a person who is interested in their input. Don't take the approach that as a manager, administer, superintendent, principal, etc., that you know more than the experienced worker. It is your job to put the pieces together, but utilize all the advice you can obtain to make decisions that will affect the majority of individuals under your supervision.

This next chapter will be my last working assignment. It will encompass approximately fourteen years and will be the best years of my working life. Finally, it will also be my self-actualization enlightenment and will serve as the final chapter in my working career.

Chapter Eight

Back to Education

School Counselor

I WAS OUT of work once again but determined to return to the educational environment in the capacity as a school counselor. I was willing to take on any assignment that would give me the experience that counseling directors were looking for and set out to contact as many school districts within a certain area that I could. My family was now living on my unemployment compensation and my wife's salary as a medical administrator.

The non-profit that I previously resigned from disputed whether I was justified in receiving the benefits from the government. I was requested by the compensation board to write a letter to advocate my need for the compensation, which I completed and sent. The government's decision was in my favor, and I was granted the unemployment compensation. If you feel that you are eligible for benefits, don't take "no" for an answer unless you have explored every avenue of eligibility.

With the need of additional income and my commitment to getting back in the educational world, I dove into the task of finding a position in a school district that would give me the chance to prove my skills as a new school counselor.

This time period was about fifteen years ago, and I was not as computer literate as now (which is still far below the younger generation), and social networking was not as prevalent as it is now. Therefore, I used computer access to find the counseling directors of every school district within a certain distance from my home. I actually wrote down each and every name of the directors, school districts, and their phone numbers. I then called each district office on my list and requested a short conversation with the counseling director. I did not always have success in reaching and speaking with the directors, but I did come away with information on whether there was a counseling position available, who to send a resumé to, and when to expect a return contact. I was applying in the middle of the school year (January), and did not necessarily expect a full-time position to be available. I was looking more for a temporary spot that would afford me the in-school experience that directors were asking for.

I was lucky enough to be called in for an interview for a position at a local high school that had an anticipated opening for a school counselor for the upcoming school year in September. The interview went well, and the director stated that he was looking for a male candidate since the other five counselors in the department were all female. He was impressed with my resumé which included my almost ten years of teaching experience and my management skills outside the educational environment. He advised me to sign up as a substitute so I would be recognized in the district as someone with counseling credentials until he was ready to interview for the counseling position.

A short time after registering with the district, an opening for a counselor in one of the three high schools in the district (not the school that I had interviewed with) was available for a three days a week assignment as a temporary position for the rest of the school year. In addition, a counseling director that I interviewed with previously from another school informed me that there was also another temporary counseling position in a high school much farther away for a two days a week position. I interviewed for both positions and was hired for both which encompassed a full week of counseling students in two different school districts.

These positions, although not the most convenient, allowed me to obtain the experience and the chance to show my skills and abilities in a counseling environment. I was on my way to establishing my career in the counseling field that I so desired. By the middle of April of the same year, the counseling director that I initially interviewed with, who was looking for a male candidate, hired me as a full-time school counselor starting in September. I was thrilled that I had changed careers and obtained a very desirable counseling position located in a high school within a short distance of my home. I had hit the jackpot in my quest for employment in a position in education that was now my true desire and one that I felt would afford me the self-actualization award that I so desperately yearned for.

I remember clearly how excited I was about the counseling position. After a short period of time, I would tell my friends that I felt that I was semi-retired. The duties of the position were substantial and kept me busy and somewhat overwhelmed, but I was performing in an environment that I enjoyed, working with students and staff that were, for the most part delightful, and I had the summers off. What a great job! The district credited my almost ten years of teaching experience and placed me on the appropriate salary step. I was also given the opportunity to add those teaching years to my pension when I retired by having deductions taken out of my salary. Financially, our family still lived paycheck to paycheck as most Americans, but I had a newfound approach to my life. I had finally landed in an awesome working environment at age fifty and felt very fortunate.

The first few years, I flourished in an environment of acceptance, appreciation, and respect. Our counseling department consisted of five female counselors that were, believe it or not, all older than I and the male director who had hired me. Some were more experienced than others, but they all had the hands-on counseling skills with teenagers and within a brief period of time, I developed and exhibited the counseling skills and abilities that I knew I possessed.

The student body was comprised of low-to middle-class, economically disadvantaged kids who, many times, were the first generation in their family to graduate high school and possibly attend college. Many of these kids came from broken families or single parent surroundings and had to overcome difficult odds to succeed. Assisting these kids through their tough times, especially as ninth and tenth graders, and witnessing their development into mature young adults as seniors, was extremely rewarding. There was an outstanding atmosphere of collaboration and friendliness within our department. The staff loved what they were doing and performed willingly the many aspects of the position.

During the early years of my counseling career, I met and became close with a student that came to our school as a sophomore, transferring due to the family relocation into our district. He was diagnosed with a debilitating cancer. He was very open about his medical issues during our first introduction with his mother in my office. Instantly, he displayed a zest for life that was easily recognizable to whomever came in contact with him. He would not allow his disease to take over his ambitions and goals, no matter how his medical outlook would determine his future. He was a warrior facing a desperate, but unknown situation.

Each year, I would sit with him and document his schedule for the following year with the classes that would be appropriate for entering college and map out the local colleges that he wanted to apply to. His grades were good, but his medical issues, especially with weekly treatments, made it difficult at times to complete assignments with what he felt were his best efforts. He would frequently come to my office asking for help with explaining to his teachers why some of his work was not up to his standards. We established a great rapport during his visits, and he looked forward to my guidance as I looked forward to his appearance at my door.

During his junior year, he applied to several colleges, and by the beginning of his senior year, was accepted to a well-known local four-year college. He was thrilled with his acceptance letter and gladly waved it at me during one of his visits at the beginning of his senior year. However, his health was deteriorating quickly, and during the middle part of his senior year, he could not function in school. I would deliver his school work to his apartment on a weekly basis and was devastated each time as I witnessed the progression of his disease and his failing health. He wanted so desperately to graduate with his class. Unfortunately, he passed halfway through his senior year and did not get the chance to walk at graduation.

For most of my life until this time, I had not known anyone close to me, neither family nor friends, who had passed away. This experience left me with a deep sorrow and a feeling I had lost something inside of me. It so happened that his passing in January of that year was the beginning of a very difficult year in my life. I lost my mom, dad, and mother-in-law all during that same year.

I was invited by his family to say a few words at his viewing, which was something I had never previously done. I clearly remember putting together on paper the few words that I intended to convey to the many people attending his viewing at his family's church. I could not read the few thoughts I had put together while in my basement without an emotional interruption. I attended the viewing with one of my colleagues who also had a bond with this student. I was extremely nervous about how I was going to be able to stand at a podium and recite words that were so sincere and emotional that each time I read them aloud, I would instantly sob.

When we entered the beautifully decorated church, I realized not only that there were many more patrons attending than I expected but also the atmosphere was presented as an uplifting ceremony honoring the life of this exceptional kid.

There was music, singing and encouragement that I had never witnessed in any other viewing that I had attended. During any of my attendance at other viewings, my Italian heritage mostly allowed only for sadness and mourning.

I was the third and last participant to be called up to the stage to relate some thoughts about the close relationship I had with this student as his counselor. The two previous speakers essentially stated some positive and humorous encounters that were remembered with kind words about their connection and friendship with the departed. My short but emotional words tended to tug at the heartstrings instead of the fond memories that the two previous speakers so eloquently evoked.

As I read each word, I attempted to stifle the emotional reactions that were rumpling inside me but needed to stop and control my speech a few times. I related the heartfelt connection we had and how much I would miss him. When it was over, I had the feeling of acceptance that I related my fervent thoughts, however sadly, to the listeners. I felt an inner gratification that I gave tribute to our student and that he would be appreciative of my sincere words.

In the audience, which I was unaware at the time, was a national radio commentator who was well-known as a radio personality to many who listened to his national broadcasts. He was there because he had a summer camp that invited young cancer patients to enjoy a couple weeks of fun and activities that he sponsored and financed. Our student had attended several summers at his camp, and he felt such a close attachment to the deceased that he flew in to attend his viewing. I was informed that he had mentioned my name along with the other speakers on one of his broadcasts and applauded our efforts and words to his loyal listeners. I knew my words for my friend were real and impassioned, but hearing this acknowledgement truly made me feel I had dignified my hero the best that I could.

This entire episode gave me a true understanding of how life can be curtailed and relationships shortened and to be grateful for the time on earth that we all have and for the exceptional people we meet during our lifetime.

The next few years came with some changes in our department due to retirement of several of the counselors in our office. In addition, the director who hired me was promoted to a high-level, district office, administrator position. A new director came to us from within the district, with a more accessible and inviting approach. She was always willingly to listen and presented a helpful and caring demeanor. She presented a true caring sensibility to the counselors under her.

The other counseling positions were filled with younger and enthusiastic individuals who exhibited the same type of nurturing and fostering approach toward the students in their respective caseloads as the three veterans of the office, which now included myself. Some interns and brief stints (a year or two) by a few extraordinary counselors made the counseling office a wonderful place to work. We would eat lunch together in a room across from our office in order to be in close proximity to the secretarial staff in case there was a need for one of us to assist a student. Our lunches were punctuated with conversations that produced joyous laughter and jokes galore. We developed a closeness that is rare in any type of office setting. We became a working family that I dubbed as the "Counselinos". Using my Italian heritage, I, of course, was the Godfather and reigned over a family which included a mother, a wife, a sister, nieces, nephews, and cousins under my tutelage. Our close-knit, family atmosphere became the envy of many of the teachers and staff at our school, and our popularity spread to the other two high schools in our district. Our building became the school of choice in the district, and we carried our family creation as badges of pride for our school.

Sometime during this tremendously rewarding time, I realized my long desired self-actualization was achieved. I have mentioned this term several times during my working career story and my true aspirations of attaining this goal. Self-actualization is a term used in counseling circles and is defined in the dictionary as: "the realization or fulfillment of an individual's talents and potentialities, especially considered as a drive or need present in everyone." I believe it is knowing who you are, what you are, and being certain if the choice is needed to be made, that you will choose the right and "good" direction rather the poor and "bad" path. Mistakes will be made and learned from, but when the important issues in life are presented, the appropriate and honorable choices will be selected.

I would often kiddingly announce to my colleagues and anyone willing to listen that, "If you don't like me, than there is something wrong with you." At first, this phrase sounds a little quirky and arrogant, but it has honestly been and remains my philosophy to this day. I feel I have acquired the experience, wisdom, and inner assurance that are needed for my self-actualization to be completed. Through the ups and downs of my long and ever-changing working career, I had realized my potential, developed my talents to the best of my ability, and was performing my duties with a sense of fulfillment. The continuous rewards from counseling and guiding our young people, and the atmosphere that was a constantly energizing reality in our office, gave me the confidence and certainty that I had achieved my goal.

Working with the students under my counseling umbrella and guiding them toward their goals only assisted in my level of perception that I had been placed in a position of great necessity. I was extremely grateful that I could, for the most part, pass on my knowledge and experience for the benefit of these wonderful young kids.

One of the important factors that counselors have is the opportunity to work with students on a one-to-one basis. With this arrangement, most students, no matter how desperate and challenging their situations can be, will at least attempt to listen and hopefully follow your guidance. Some will be very difficult to reach but will eventually "get it," and then some will be unreachable due to situations beyond the counselor's scope. However, the youth are our future, and we can only hope that they don't make the same mistakes that the previous generation have made. We must guide them in the right direction, teach them right from wrong, counsel them to be kind to others, hope they conduct themselves honorably and that their path in life will be a successful one. Parents should be their mentors, teachers and counselors their advisors, family and friends their choice to follow or not and their personal framework to choose their pathway to their own self-actualization.

As our department continued with a camaraderie that made each day a pleasure to come to work, defining developments were happening without our knowledge that would drastically change the history of our school. One of my colleagues coined these somewhat earth-shattering matters as "ground zero" in the downfall of the school's reputation and prominence. A sex scandal exploded into our school's world.

After summer vacation, sometime within the middle years of my tenure, the entire faculty met for our welcome back meeting. During that meeting, we noticed a popular teacher's absence and heard the beginning stages of some rumors surrounding the staff but not with any substantial or confirmed information. We heard that the missing teacher had been fired but had no idea why he was fired.

Eventually, the rumors became clearer, and some unbelievable gossip became reality. Once the school year began and the kids were in classes, another male teacher suddenly vanished under similar suggestions of some type of student/teacher misconduct. When a third male teacher was handcuffed and removed from the school's field during a gym practice, we then began hearing tons of slanderous news from within the school. In addition, the media caught on that a sex scandal had occurred within the jurisdiction of our school with three male teachers and three female students.

The media swarmed over our school's grounds daily. Every day during that time, we would look through our office windows, which gave us a wide view of the front of the school, to see the various local TV crews with their large trucks and strategically placed cameras filming the school's building. News reporters were hoping to get some dialogue from any staff or student willing to be interviewed.

Several times, as I walked in or was leaving the building, a reporter would approach me asking some questions about the now infamous situation that occurred at our school. Of course, we were instructed by our administration not to speak with the media. It was our personal decision to not give out any information, especially since we were so removed from any wrongdoing and still hadn't grasped all that was being implied by the media.

As the cases were taken over by law enforcement, the TV reports which were now receiving national coverage, blatantly disclosed to the public that an awareness of sexual encounters were permeated throughout the school as permissible behavior by some of the staff and administration. I found this reporting to be disturbing and completely untrue. Most of what we were aware of revolved around the knowledge that three male teachers had some type of inappropriate sexual actions with three separate female students that occurred over the past year or so. We were also informed that one of the students confided in a substitute teacher who felt the need to "blow the whistle" and inform the authorities. Our entire department and most of the school's staff viewed the decision of this "sub" as a positive development due to her resolve and purposefulness to relay the improper behavior of these teachers to the authorities in order to help the student. It was looked upon as a tremendously courageous response by a young teacher. (This staff member was employed by the district but taught at another high school.)

Two of the three female students were in my caseload, and I knew them well. Over the four years that we were together, I easily assessed that they were both great kids from good families and were very interested in their future goals. I did not know the third student, but it is my sincere belief that the students did no wrong, and every misdeed was the fault of these three despicable male teachers. They took advantage of these vulnerable, impressionable young teenagers, and in various ways, violated them. I knew the two girls as very respectable, conscientious, and intense about their education and future aspirations, and I was convinced that they were caught up with unethical adults who took advantage of their youth and manipulated them. Some of their teacher counterparts actually were more sympathetic toward these contemptible teacher comrades than the students, which just boggled my mind.

No matter how flirtatious or extreme the behavior of any teenager toward an adult, there is no excuse or valid logic that would permit the adult to sexually engage the teen, especially as their teachers or mentors. I know there are laws in our country that the age of consensual sex varies by state. However, adults must adhere to proper standards because they should know better and in order for our society to function in a civil matter.

On a daily basis, detectives would be seen in the hallways and in the main office. Each day would be filled with, "What will happen next?" During a year or so after the allegations were confirmed, the hammer came down on a vice-principal and the principal of our school, who were permanently removed, and reached far into the district with the resignation of the superintendent.

While all of this was happening, our counseling department remained intact and a refuge from the craziness that surrounded our building. Our director, however, was pulled into the fray by being one of the few supervising staff members willing to make difficult decisions without a principal. Even when the district brought on a temporary principal, her responsibilities continued to increase to the point that it was affecting her ability to continue to supervise our department.

Luckily, our staff recognized her contributions to our school and was able to function on our own. The attempt to keep the staff, parents, the community, and the students calm and on track was overwhelming.

Eventually, in my opinion, our director became disillusioned with her responsibilities and decided to take a promotion to the district office. This was viewed by our department as a positive development for her personal well-being but a definite loss to our department and the "family" that we conceived. In addition, it was now time for the district's administration to bring in a new principal who would then hire a new counseling director. It was a time that changes would affect everyone in our department and most of the staff of our school.

The administration members of our district, which included a new superintendent, decided to hire an in-district supervisor as the new principal of our school. It is my understanding that their viewpoint was that the school needed a strict and authoritative figure to come in and straighten out the public perception that the school was in dire straits and certainly no longer the school of choice within the district—for students or teachers. Therefore, a strong, no-nonsense individual was hired as principal to turn around the negative consciousness of everyone associated with the school. I have had past work experiences that were relayed in this narrative with new management coming in to take over, and hopefully, improve the atmosphere. The past examples were not successful to my well-being, and this change over was no exception.

The new principal came in with a "guns a blazing" mentality. Changes were made, departments restructured, and rules enforced but with no sense of coordination or collaboration with the staff. It was a difficult beginning for most.

I have related within this narrative about management style and my preference toward working with others to implement and improve a working environment. My feeling and experience lends to the approach of consulting with staff, finding solutions with input from experienced and front line personnel, collaborating when making changes, and creating an atmosphere of mutual respect in making decisions that will affect the entire operation. This is the mindset I would use as a new manager entering any type of organization, even more so with an educational setting. However the above approach was not the choice of the incoming principal. Whether it was from the administration at the district level or the personal decision of the principal, the management direction was much more authoritative and much less interested in teamwork, than I would have implemented in my professional opinion.

From the beginning, my connection with the new principal was not a good one simply because I felt my background and experience in management (not known by anyone) had proved successful. It was easy to see why this person was selected as the new principal. She had many positive attributes. Dedication to the position, very knowledgeable in the complexities of dealing with the public, extremely computer literate, intelligent, and experienced in education law that had become more restrictive over the years were all qualities that she possessed. However, I felt her ability to properly communicate with the staff, her forceful, demanding actions, and her disparaging demeanor were not the most affective way to lead.

Respect for management should be gained by having mutual appreciation of an individual's efforts and experience and a willingness to realize that the manager's understanding may not always be the best approach. Egos and self-absorption should not be part of the manager's mindset. Too often with this situation, it was "my way or the highway" without discussion or explanation. If you disagreed, you were shunned as a non-conformist. If you made a mistake, you were incompetent.

The management style became one of fear of retaliation and a desire to hide from any controversy, which was the choice of many of the staff. The last few years of my tenure as a counselor, after I decided my time to retire, was to take the approach of performing my duties and guiding my students with as little as possible contact with the school's administration. Of course, it was inevitable that I would "get in trouble" for things sometimes out of my control and was reprimanded a few times. In addition, a new counseling director was hired for our department who came with some experience, but not the type that would enable her to confront an egotistical, dictator-style of management. Often times, our director would be micro-managed and bull-dozed by the principal into decisions that might not be in the best interest of our department or staff. The new counseling director eventually resigned after three years of relentless interference by the principal and was hired by another school district in the area. She has since gone on to be very successful and well appreciated by her new school.

At the end of the second year of this principal's reign, our department was to lose a partial counseling position to another school in the district. A decision was needed to be made to have one counselor share time at two of the district's high schools. Because of the complexity and possible confusion of having a caseload of students in each school and commuting back and forth every other day, no one in our department wanted to be selected. Even though I was higher than others in seniority, I was the choice for this position. I assumed it was the decision of the principal to choose me due to my past indiscretions, but others also informed me that I was chosen because the administration thought I could best handle the intricacies of the situation. Either way, I was apprehensive about the move initially, but after some adjustment; I realized it was a positive development for my counseling career.

I clearly witnessed a change in management style at the school that I was now a part-time counselor. The principal, who was well respected by the staff and a veteran in her position, would delegate responsibilities to the appropriate supervisors and would be extremely competent in performing her duties. She would be a welcome sight for the staff at whatever functions she would lead. The supervisors, in turn, would use her guidance to implement and coordinate their departments with a confidence that the principal was always on their side and had their "back." Personally, she would always say "hi" and ask how I was doing whenever we would meet in the hallway, even though I was not a regular at the school. I felt this was a kind gesture toward someone new to the building and appreciated her acknowledgement. The management style that I had used during my working career was definitely alive in this high school environment and functioning quite nicely.

I seemed to be able to miss out on faculty meetings and other adverse situations that occurred at my home school by attending my duties as a new counselor at the new school. The students at the new school were the same type of outstanding and engaging kids I counseled at my home school. The counseling director at the new school exhibited a helpful and supportive approach in our department and a true sense of caring for the counselors under his supervision. The schoolteachers and staff were friendly and attentive. My part-time stay at this school that now was the school of choice within the district was an overwhelming positive experience. By the end of the year, I felt very fortunate that I was the one chosen for this assignment.

However before the end of the year (I would have two more years before retirement), I was informed by the principal of my home school that I would be assigned to this new school permanently for the next school year. Normally, I would have welcomed this transfer. However, since I was so close to retirement and having close relationships with several students that I counseled over the last several years, my desire to remain at my home school, even with all of its distractions, was strong. In addition, two counselors in our department and I who were together from day one had developed a very close working relationship over the years. (We were still "family.") They would be retiring the year that I would have been transferred.

I met with the principal and explained my reasons for wanting to remain at my home school. I was informed that the decision, according to the administration, had been made, and there was not much I could do about it. In addition, both the principal and the counseling director at the new school requested my services because they were very pleased with my performance as a part-time counselor. The next day, my two trusted colleagues and long time friends appealed to the principal, and the decision to transfer me was rescinded. I was to continue at the school that I began my counseling career for the last two years of my working life. I would also remain with my two counseling comrades for their last year before retirement. I certainly appreciated the acknowledgements from the principal and director from the other school and explained to both why I wanted to stay at the home school after the decision was re-voked. I reiterated to them my true appreciation for the time I attended their school and thanked them for their support.

Before I continue with my last year of my working life, I must in-clude my time and involvement with our union/association. During the several years of my time as a school counselor, there was disillusionment within the staff about a previous contract that was negotiated by the union with the district's board members. There was a long and drawn out time frame when the contract discussions were interrupted for whatever reason. The contract had to be concluded by an arbitrator who ruled in favor of the union, and the pact was ratified by the membership.

However, the overall opinion including my viewpoint was that the contract could have been better. The governor of our state (who we all despised) was against unions and tried to control any advances or gains that associations had made in the past. Teachers complained continu-ously about the contract and about the lack of communication from the union with the members. I, too, complained, but also wanted to find out how the union process worked.

Another contract was ratified without the contentious dealings of the previous contract. (Contracts usually extend for three years' dura-tion.) When the next contract was within a year of completion or stall-ing, I decided to join a committee and attempt to find out the inner structure of the union and what, if anything, I could contribute to the process.

During my involvement with the committee, I became friendly with a teacher who was moving up in stature within the union. He soon became an officer of the association and automatically was issued a seat at the negotiation table for the next upcoming contract. I relayed to him my past experiences with unions during my working career and also my desire to be part of the negotiation committee. I not only wanted to be part of the process, but felt I could add to the team due to my varied background.

Before any proceedings with actual negotiation, I was chosen as one of the non-officer spots on the union's negotiation team. I attended several association-sponsored classes in order to be prepared for the negotiating procedures and developments. We met as a team several times before the actual bargaining meetings began in order to strategize our points and prepare for the opposite views of the district's team. When the time came for the actual face-to-face proceedings, we felt confident and ready for whatever the other side would present to us. There were a few members of our team that were experienced veterans of several rounds of past negotiating sessions. We heavily relied on their knowledge and expertise and became a cohesive unit before entering the "arena." We had a lawyer steeped in union negotiation on our side and the district had the counterpart lawyer on their side. During the meetings, only the lawyers for each side and one individual selected from each side were to verbally discuss the issues surrounding the contract. A document was presented to the district as a beginning proposal to consider. In addition, the state provided a mediator to oversee the proceedings.

We had a few non-productive sessions with the district's team who initially provided us with a ridiculously insufficient counter-offer. Finally, after several additional conferences, both sides concluded with a mutually agreed package that would be formulated into a contract to be presented to the union membership.

It was interesting to witness how the district's initial offer, which was inadequate and almost insulting, changed to a much more palatable, acceptable, and fair presentation at the end. Why begin a negotiating round with such an inferior approach that they know will aggravate the already tense atmosphere of "us against them" mentality? It reminded me of the typical auto salesman giving a outrageously high initial price on a car and then coming down to a much lower figure in order to get you to buy the car before you leave the showroom. Why not negotiate closer from the beginning to avoid the negative perception that this type of bargaining will only serve to "stir the pot"? I have witnessed and have been informed by experienced negotiators that the "low-ball" pathway is by far the norm. I just don't understand why!!!!

The contract, which our team felt was an appropriate step forward for our union, was overwhelmingly ratified by the membership. This entire experience left me with a positive impression of the union purpose, especially in an education setting. (As I presented previously in this narrative, I did not always have that connection with other union episodes in my working life.) The following school year, I resigned my position on the negotiating team due to my close proximity to my retirement. I encouraged others to join in the efforts of the union and recommended involvement and participation.

The school year before my retirement year was uneventful for the most part; except for the continuing captivating student exchanges and excellent rapport building with the kids within my caseload and some that were frequent visitors to our department. Most of the year, my two counselor buddies and I attempted to hide from any controversy and avoid the administration as much as we could. My compatriots were counting down the days when they would retire and be free of the disturbances of our school. As the school year approached its final days, we celebrated their retirement with the hope that we would continue our friendship and stay in contact for many years after. In addition to losing my two closest confidants, our counseling director's resignation happened at the end of the same year. I was left in my last school year with a department of counselors, some new, some seasoned, that I had no true connection with and a new counseling director.

The final year of my working life began with a positive sense that I could make it basically on my own by concentrating on a new caseload of students and maintaining a low profile within my department. The new director seemed to be a nice guy and knowledgeable but with a "self promoting personality".

Since my realization of attaining my self-actualization goal, I not only sustain an inner self-confidence but also an aptitude for recognizing both the good in others, and likewise, their negative aspects. In most cases, within a short period of time, I am able to assess an individual's tendencies and come up with a clear grasp of their true intentions. I am normally "spot on" when figuring out an individual's objectives.

The first month or so went smoothly, and the director and counseling staff worked together to implement any changes he felt were necessary for improving the department. Although the director was open to our suggestions and observations, he let it be known early on that "his way" would be the only way and that we were to adjust to his approaches whether we agreed or disagreed. Since this was my final year, I only questioned some situations but quickly realized that I was better off just following his lead.

New supervisors coming into an established environment certainly have the right to come in with their own ideas and concepts but should also listen and coordinate the opinions of the existing staff that may or may not have better or different approaches. The new director was much more interested in conveying and completing the wishes of the principal/administration whether their direction was considered the right path or not.

Several supervisors that I have known tend to have blinders on, whether they are new or seasoned, whenever instructions/directives are funneled down to the masses from the administrators in charge. There are many times, as I have communicated in this narrative, that the administrators/authorities are not only incorrect in their assumptions but sometimes are so far removed from the front line that their mandates are not conducive to their entity, especially in the education setting. The supervisors very rarely question or examine the commands from above but simply pass on the edicts for implementation. There does not seem to be any opposition at any level in the current educational realm from the individuals that could make a difference. Upon realizing the director's approach, I was determined to follow along and hopefully get through the year unscathed.

A few months into my final year, I became very sick and was out of school for about a month. I had developed severe sepsis from a stent that was implanted to flush out a kidney stone (sorry for the graphic description). After I was out of danger and recuperating in the hospital, I was informed that I could have died from the complications if the condition was not treated properly. When you go through a life-threatening episode such as this, and are at my age, you begin to concentrate on what are the most important things in your life.

When I returned to work, my focus was much more on my family and future life rather than my duties as a counselor. I continued to give everything to the students in my caseload but now began to withdraw from any attachments with the counseling staff and especially the director. During my illness, I only received a few texts from the director, mostly about the condition of my health. I did not receive any card or acknowledgements from anyone in our counseling office during my month-long absence. When I returned, I again did not receive any "welcome back" recognition from the counseling staff, only inquires of what had happened.

What a difference from when there was a "family" atmosphere several years back in the counseling office. I fondly remember when I had a knee replacement a few years back, which of course was not life threatening, that besides the many cards and gifts, several of the counselors and our director came to my home and had lunch with me in order to make me feel better and to confirm that they cared for my well being. As I realized more and more that I was basically alone in our department, and that the director was looking more toward the future and my replacement, I began counting the days till my retirement.

The last few months of my tenure as a counselor did seem to go by quickly. As the end came closer, several staff members would acknowledge my good fortunes to come and would converse in a much more friendly nature. The few future retirees and myself bonded in the acceptance that our time for a change in lifestyle was about to happen. The counseling staff also became more engaged in my eventual retirement and planned a lovely dinner out with gifts for my up coming departure. We connected by reminiscing past humorous events and how much we enjoyed them. Thankfully, my current director did not attend, but our previous director who was part of our "family" from the past, did attend. We had reconnected my last week or so with an exit interview that she conducted which was more of a "look back" to the good old times then an actual interview.

My last week, which was anticipated but downplayed, began with my attempt to say farewell to as many teachers, administrators, and non-teaching staff that I felt some sort of a connection with during my years at the school, and I wished them all well. I also returned for a "goodbye" session with the other school that I had spent a half-year with and felt a sincere attachment to many of the staff.

When my last day came, I was more than ready to depart and begin a new phase of my life. I left without hesitation, regret, or sadness. The fond memories of my counseling time will always be a part of me, but the closeness and attachment to the counseling office personnel had left me a year or so ago. However, I will always have a place in my heart for the special kids that came in to my life during my counseling career and the many close relationships we developed. I counseled so many great kids and hope they are all having successful lives, but there are a few that will be forever a part of me. There is one very special youngster who overcame tremendous odds as a freshman to become a delightful well-adjusted young lady as a senior that hopefully will go on to accomplish her lofty aspirations. Even now, we still refer to each other as father and daughter whenever we infrequently connect via social media.

The final phase of my working life has ended. Although I will write another chapter below about my now wonderful life in retirement, I have completed and relayed over fifty years of my working life. I have made some mistakes and have had several negative occurrences happen over the years, but I truly feel that, if I did not go through the difficult times, that I would not be the fulfilled individual I am today.

Yes, many times things could have gone a little easier, but I have grown, matured, and become self-confident through the circumstances that surrounded my working life. I successfully achieved my ultimate goal of self-actualization, and I am secure in who I am and what I will be in the future. Good luck to all who will take on the challenge to attempt to achieve your self-actualization objective.

Chapter Nine

Retirement

MY RETIREMENT HAS been nothing short of fantastic so far. I did not make a tremendous amount of money during my working life (I still view my checkbook almost daily), but with pensions and social security, my wife and I are living comfortably and feel blessed that we can spend our latter years enjoying this next phase of our lives hopefully for many, many years to come. I often state that I got paid all those years for working and now get paid for not working!! Life is good.

Whether you are just starting out or somewhere in the middle, try your best to save for future years. If you are in education, don't let the government or any other entity take away your pension. Join your union and fight to keep what educators deserve for their post teaching days. Whether you stay at one place in your career for a long period of time, which is becoming more obsolete, or move around much like myself, be sure to have direction in assisting in financial avenues for your eventual retirement. If you are living day-to-day at a job and cannot salvage a small amount for your future, then find another job. Look into several suggestions I related in this book, and no matter how difficult this challenge may seem, take the positive approach, and attempt to reach your potential.

My wife and I were fortunate enough to invest in a property in Florida and now spend the winters in the warmth of the sunshine state. We have the best of both worlds with the weather, and we maintain our family and friends connections with our peeps at home in New Jersey and Philadelphia.

At this point in my life, I have had very little or no contact with most of the individuals that I have met during my working journey. I would love to somehow reconnect with the "good" ones and would be happy to never be in contact with the "not so good" ones. I lost all, or most, of any communication with my last and most recent position where I spent the last fourteen years of my life. I hope that morale has improved and that the administration is headed in the right direction. However, I am very pleased to relate that my two counseling comrades that I mentioned in the previous chapter have continued to bond our friendship with lunches and social media correspondence. We also have an additional counselor who worked with us for a couple of years and was a member of the "family" as part of our foursome of really good friends. He is much younger than the three of us but has a mature soul that connects with us in many different ways. I hope our relationships will continue for many more years.

My wife and I also decided to follow our entrepreneur spirit and delved into the antique and collectable arena by opening a small retail unit in a large warehouse-type setting in order to make an additional few bucks after retirement.

The end result, although enjoyable while it lasted, produced little or no additional income and basically became a pleasurable hobby. However, we realized a creativity and talent that we did not recognize as part of our nature. We would look for and obtain dilapidated pieces of furniture at yard sales and flea markets and turn them into attractive and desirable items that we would then sell at our retail space. It was fun and interesting, for the most part, but became somewhat of a burden to continue to find the right inventory and the time to produce the exceptional pieces that was our forte. We gave it up prior to leaving for Florida and have no intentions of continuing in any capacity. After all, retirement is doing what you want to do, when you want to, and enjoying every minute.

I continue to develop my self-actualization by knowing what I have accomplished, realizing my strengths and weaknesses, and striving to continue to be the best person I know. Due to my age, I have become more cognizant of my existence and my time left on earth. I have good "age" genes in my family and hope to live for a long time. However, there is no secret to longevity. I pray daily for continued good health for my family and friends and a long life for all within my circle. I have attempted to pay it forward with passing on the successes and pitfalls of my working life, hoping to help others with their search for meaningful employment. In addition, I have shared management and supervisory styles that I have witnessed and incorporated during my career employment that centered in developing mutual cooperation with employee and employer. I have also provided styles of authority that I did not agree with and attempted to explain my reasoning. I confidently believe I have produced the best representation of my working life to everyone that reads this manuscript.

If you have recognized any part of this narrative and feel there is a connection, feel free to contact me through the various social communication avenues. I would love to reconnect and listen to your thoughts.

I hope you enjoyed reading my work journey and its description. Please pass on its relevance to anyone you feel may benefit by the contents. Best wishes for reaching your fullest potential.

34583765R10097

Made in the USA
Middletown, DE
27 January 2019